A to Z 神秘案件

中英双语

第一辑

The Haunted Hotel
酒店奇异事件

[美] 罗恩·罗伊 著
[美] 约翰·史蒂文·格尼 绘 曹幼南 译

人物介绍

三人小组的成员，聪明勇敢，喜欢读推理小说，紧急关头总能保持头脑冷静。喜欢在做事之前好好思考！

丁丁

三人小组的成员，活泼机智，喜欢吃好吃的食物，常常有意想不到的点子。

乔希

三人小组的成员，活泼开朗，喜欢从头到脚穿同一种颜色的衣服，总是那个能找到大部分线索的人。

露丝

斯皮韦茨太太

酒店的主人，非常热爱香格里拉酒店，不愿意酒店被卖掉。为了查清楚酒店的风波，让孩子们免费入住酒店调查真相。

杰弗斯先生

酒店的客人，自称曾经见过出现在酒店中的鬼。酒店风波之后，仅有的两位没有搬走的客人之一。

杰弗斯太太

酒店的客人，自称曾经见过出现在酒店中的鬼。酒店风波之后，仅有的两位没有搬走的客人之一。

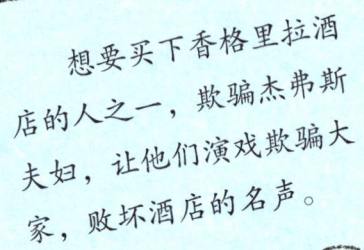

想要买下香格里拉酒店的人之一,欺骗杰弗斯夫妇,让他们演戏欺骗大家,败坏酒店的名声。

弗莱彻·易奇

想要买下香格里拉酒店的人之一,欺骗杰弗斯夫妇,让他们演戏欺骗大家,败坏酒店的名声。

伦道夫·雷尔

想要买下香格里拉酒店的人之一,欺骗杰弗斯夫妇,让他们演戏欺骗大家,败坏酒店的名声。

迈尔斯·鲁克

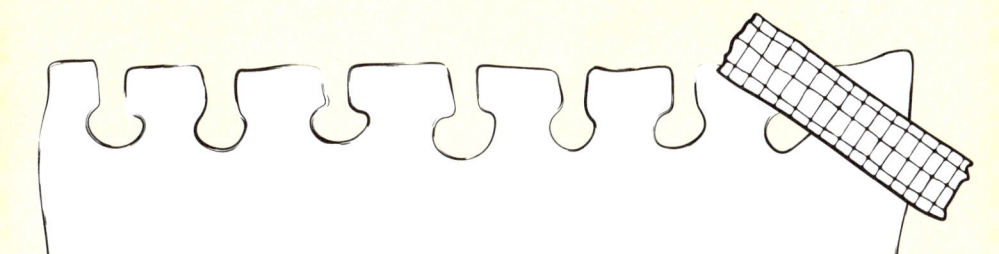

字母 H 代表 horror，恐怖……

"但有一点我很清楚，"丁丁说，"要是让我插手，没有鬼能将香格里拉酒店闹得关门！"

"丁丁说得对。"露丝说，"林克莱特先生是我们的朋友，我们必须想想办法！"

突然，电梯门开了，一个白色身影站在那里看着他们。

"鬼！"乔希尖叫起来。

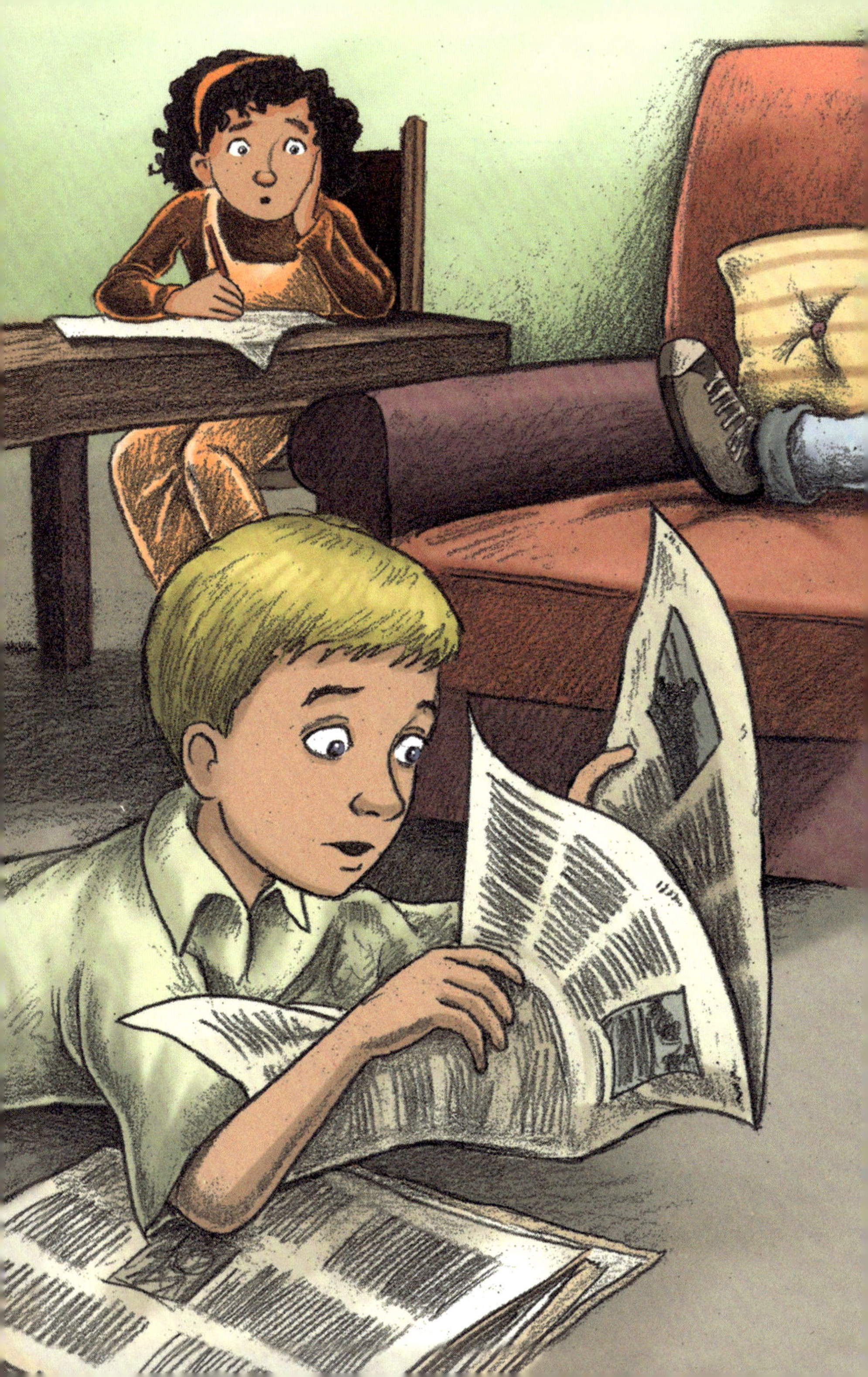

第一章

"噢,天哪!"丁丁叫道,"绿地镇有鬼!"

唐纳德·戴维·邓肯——朋友们都叫他丁丁——此时正趴在客厅的地板上翻看周日的报纸。

乔希躺在沙发上,正用葡萄干教丁丁的豚鼠洛蕾塔算术。

洛蕾塔狼吞虎咽地吃掉了其中一粒葡萄干。

"洛蕾塔！"乔希训斥它，"如果你总是把葡萄干吃掉，你永远也学不会加法！"

露丝正在做填字游戏。"也许它正在试图教你减法，乔希。"她说。

乔希朝她掷了一粒葡萄干。

"我是认真的，你们两个！"丁丁指着《绿地报》的头版新闻说，"快来看看这个！"

露丝扫了一眼报纸后大声叫道："嘿，是林克莱特先生！"

乔希把洛蕾塔放回笼子里，然后站在丁丁身后看了看报纸上的新闻标题：

闹鬼的酒店！鬼吓跑了香格里拉酒店的客人

"看吧，就像我刚说的那样。"丁丁说。

乔希的脸上露出了笑容。"你不会真的相信吧？"他问，"我打赌这不过是万圣节的玩笑。"

"也许吧，但是照片里的林克莱特先生似乎很不开心。"丁丁说，"再说他从不开玩笑！"

"而且，万圣节离现在还有两周呢。"露丝补充道。

乔希哼了一声。"我可不相信这世上有鬼，"他说，"除非我亲眼看见！"

"你们听听这一段。"丁丁读起报纸上的内容，"'客人们声称午夜时分有鬼飘过走廊，那只鬼还拿着一把银光闪闪的剑！'"

乔希又哼了一声。"鬼是不会拿剑的。"他说。

露丝伸手拿起她的夹克，说："我们为什么不去酒店亲眼看一看呢？"

"好主意。"丁丁说着，穿上了运动鞋。

乔希长长地叹了一口气，说："好吧，我只是去证明我是对的。"

孩子们离开了丁丁家，朝银环路走去。

一群孩子正在绿地小学踢足球。他们的鼻子红红的，丁丁看见他们呼出的气体形成了白雾。操场周围的树木已经变成了红色和金黄色。

主街上，两根电线杆之间挂着一条长长的横幅。横幅上用醒目的文字写着：

红叶周（10月13日—10月20日），
绿地镇欢迎您来欣赏秋天的绚丽
多彩！

孩子们到了香格里拉酒店的对面。
"看！"丁丁叫道。
　　人们拖着行李箱从酒店里拥了出来，其中一个女人还穿着拖鞋！粉红色的毛绒拖鞋上有一双兔子耳朵。

一位报社记者试图采访正要离开酒店的客人。

"您好。"她拦住一个男人说,"我是《绿地报》的琳达·戈麦斯,请问您对酒店闹鬼的传闻有什么看法?"

"无可奉告!"男人不耐烦地答道,然后急匆匆地走开了。

"让她来采访我们吧。"乔希低声说,"也许我们的名字能上报纸!"

"我们还什么都不知道呢。"丁丁说,"走吧,我们去找林克莱特先生。"

三个孩子穿过街道,从拥挤的门口挤了进去。酒店内,林克莱特先生正站在前台后面,听着一对男女抱怨。

"我们要求退款!"女人说,"我们是来这里看红叶的,不是来受惊吓的!"

林克莱特先生叹了口气。丁丁注意到他的头发乱糟糟的,眼里满是红血丝。

"当然,卡拉瑟斯太太,"林克莱特先生说,"你们将获得整周的退款。很抱歉给你们带来不好的体验,我们香格里拉酒店之前从没有闹过鬼!"

这对夫妻拎着行李箱从孩子们身边匆匆走过,然后从门口挤了出去。

"天哪,他们好像很生气。"乔希说。

"我们去和林克莱特先生谈一谈。"丁丁说。

正在这时,电话铃响了,林克莱特先生转身去接电话。

"等等,那是莉薇。"露丝说,"不知道她是否了解点什么。"

莉薇·纽金特正用吸尘器清理电梯附近的地

毯。她穿着白色的工作服，系着深蓝色的围裙。

"嘿，莉薇！"露丝打招呼。

莉薇的脸上露出笑容，她关闭了吸尘器的电源。"露丝！上一次见你时，酒店发生了绑架案。现在，这里正在闹鬼！"

"我们在报纸上看到了。"露丝说，"是真的吗？"

"客人们肯定认为是真的！"莉薇说，"从周五晚上开始，这里就变得乱糟糟的。这是我们一年中最重要的一周，而客人却不断离开！"

乔希听完忍不住笑了。"是不是那只鬼突然跳出来,喊了一声'砰'?"他问。

"乔希不相信有鬼。"露丝解释。

"你相信吗?"莉薇问露丝。

露丝耸耸肩。"我不知道,但的确有东西把客人吓跑了。"

"你看见那只鬼了吗?"丁丁问。

莉薇摇了摇头,说:"没有,幸好没有。鬼出现时,我不在这儿!"

这时,林克莱特先生挂断电话,走了过来。"纽金特女士,请继续工作。"他对莉薇说。

然后他转头看向三个孩子,问道:"有什么我能帮上忙的吗,孩子们?"

"我们看到了酒店闹鬼的消息。"丁丁说。

乔希翻了个白眼。

"我们也看见客人都离开了。"露丝说。

林克莱特先生眼神悲伤,视线来回扫过酒店大堂。所有的客人都走了,大堂里空空荡荡。

林克莱特叹了一口气。"显然有只鬼吓跑了我们的客人。"他说。

"也许我们能帮上忙。"丁丁说,"您还记得那件事吗?当时您怀疑沃利斯·华莱士被绑架了,但后来我们找到了她。"

"我永远也忘不了。"林克莱特先生说道。他看着三个孩子,稀疏的小胡子颤了颤,悲伤的眼睛眯了眯。

最后他说:"请跟我来。"然后转身大步离开。

第二章

　　林克莱特先生领着孩子们走进他的办公室。他的办公室不大,里面只有一张桌子和三把椅子。房间的一面墙上挂着一幅画,画的是这家酒店。桌子上放着一个相框,相框里是一对老夫妇的照片。

　　"请坐。"林克莱特先生说。

　　孩子们坐下。林克莱特先生打开桌子的一个

抽屉，拿出一个纸袋。

"要来颗薄荷糖吗？"他问。

孩子们每人从纸袋里拿了一颗，放进了嘴里。

林克莱特先生向纸袋里看了一眼，然后往自己嘴里也放了一颗。

他靠到椅子后背上。"太糟糕了。"他说。

"我的味道还行。"乔希说,"好像是柠檬味的。"

露丝用胳膊肘碰了碰乔希。"我想他说的是那只鬼。"

乔希脸红了。"哦,不好意思。"

"我刚才说了,"林克莱特先生继续说,"这一切开始于两天前的周五。将近午夜时分,我正要关上办公室的门,一位客人跑进了大堂,大叫着三楼有鬼!"

"她有没有说鬼长什么样子?"丁丁问。

林克莱特先生抚了抚头发回答:"她说那只鬼除了眼睛的位置上是两个黑洞,其余部分都是白色的!"

三个孩子面面相觑,乔希的嘴巴张得大大的。

林克莱特先生揉了揉太阳穴,一副头痛的模样。"总之,"他接着说,"那位客人退房离开了。昨晚,更多的客人看见了鬼。它再一次出现在午夜。今天,所有的客人都退房离开了。"

林克莱特先生摇着头说:"这只鬼正在摧毁我们的生意!"

"有没有客人说那只鬼事后去了哪里?"露

丝问。

"显然它是飘走了，消失不见了。"他回答。

"您也见到那只鬼了吗？"丁丁问。

"没有。我上了楼，只看见十几个吓坏了的客人！"

林克莱特先生拿起桌子上那对老夫妇的照片。"这是我的姑妈和姑父，弗洛伦斯·斯皮韦茨和埃比尼泽·斯皮韦茨。自四十七年前他们结婚起，这家香格里拉酒店就归他们所有。"

他看着孩子们。"他们非常担心。如果这个闹鬼事件继续下去，我不知道酒店会怎么样。"

房间内出现短暂的沉默。最后，林克莱特先生站了起来。

"现在，请允许我失陪一下。"他说，"我必须去告诉姑妈和姑父，香格里拉酒店今年不会有红叶周了。"

孩子们向林克莱特先生道谢后，走回大堂。

"伙伴们，我们必须做点什么！"丁丁低声说。

"但是我们能做什么呢？"露丝问。

这时，莉薇急急忙忙朝他们走来。"他说了什么？"她问。

"他告诉了我们那只鬼的事。"露丝将林克莱特先生的话向莉薇复述了一遍。

"所以酒店里的确有鬼！"莉薇说着，不安地四处看了看，"林克莱特先生决定怎么做？"

"我不知道。"丁丁回答完，看向乔希和露丝，"但我们会尽力帮忙，对吧？"

"祝你们好运！"莉薇说，"我现在去我的小隔间吃午餐。"

她打开电梯旁边的一扇小门，消失在门里。

"我们要怎么帮忙呢？"乔希问丁丁，"我们对鬼一无所知！"

"但有一点我很清楚，"丁丁说，"要是让我插手，没有鬼能将香格里拉酒店闹得关门！"

"丁丁说得对。"露丝说，"林克莱特先生是我们的朋友，我们必须想想办法！"

突然，电梯门开了，一个白色身影站在那里看着他们。

"鬼！"乔希尖叫起来。

第三章

三个孩子呆若木鸡地站在那里,看着电梯门再次合上。

有片刻时间,三个人都没动。然后,露丝伸手按下了向上的电梯按钮。

"你做什么?"乔希尖叫道。

"跟上那只鬼。"她说。

"你疯了吗?"乔希问,"鬼要是不喜欢小孩怎么办?"

"天哪,乔希,"丁丁说,"我记得你不相信有鬼。"

"'除非我亲眼看见'。"乔希说,"而我刚刚就亲眼看见了!我们离开这里!"电梯门开了。

"太晚了,乔希。"丁丁说完,和露丝拉着乔希进了电梯。

丁丁按了去二楼的按钮。"我们一层一层检查。"他说。

二楼到了,电梯门开了,走廊是空的。

"还有两层。"露丝说着,按下了三楼的按钮。

但是他们在三楼和四楼也没有看见鬼。

"没有其他楼层了。"丁丁看着电梯按钮面板说。

"很好,我们回家吧!"乔希说。

"这个按钮有什么用?"露丝指着面板上没有数字的黑色按钮问。

"也许是紧急按钮。"丁丁说。

露丝摇了摇头说:"不是,这个红色按钮是紧急按钮。"

丁丁耸耸肩。"只有一个办法能找出答案。"他说着，按下了黑色按钮。电梯发出嘎吱嘎吱声，开始缓慢向上运行。

"我是在做噩梦，"乔希嘟哝道，"不是真的在酒店里追鬼。我随时都会醒来，醒来时我会发现自己在床上。"

"别担心，乔希。"露丝笑着说，"我会保护你的。"

电梯发出一声轻响，停了下来。

门开了，那只"鬼"正等着他们。

"它跟着我们！"乔希尖叫着，跳到了露丝身后。

"不是，是你们跟着我！""鬼"说，"你们想干什么？"

白色身影的后面，一扇门开了。一个弓着背、头发花白的男人来到走廊。

那只"鬼"用一根干瘦的手指指着孩子们说："他们跟着我来了这里，埃比尼泽。"

男人轻笑出声，慢吞吞地走向开着门的电梯。"嗯，也许我们应该把他们留下！"

緊急按鈕

"不要!"乔希从露丝身后大声叫道,"请让我们离开!"

丁丁盯着白色的身影。他之前在哪里见过这张脸呢?突然,他想起来了,她就是林克莱特先生桌子上那个相框里的女人。

丁丁走出电梯。"你们好,斯皮韦茨先生和太太。"他说,"我是丁丁·邓肯,他们是我的朋友乔希和露丝。"

"你们好。"男人一边说着,一边仔细端详着丁丁,他的眼睛是蓝莓色的,"你们一定是我侄子提过的那三个孩子。"

乔希从露丝身后偷偷看向斯皮韦茨太太。"你的意思是,她不是鬼?"他问。

"我当然不是鬼!"斯皮韦茨太太说,"埃比尼泽,我们能邀请这三个孩子进去吃点饼干吗?"

"当然,亲爱的。"老先生朝着孩子们露出了微笑,"来吧,孩子们!"

孩子们跟着斯皮韦茨老夫妇穿过一条狭窄的走廊,走进一个老式的客厅。

阳光洒满房间。透过高大的窗户,孩子们可

以看见主街对面的树梢。

丁丁环顾房间,墙上挂满了画,还放着很多书——他从来没有见过这么多书!

斯皮韦茨太太端着一个盘子走了进来。"请坐。"她对孩子们说着,递给每个孩子一杯牛奶。斯皮韦茨先生拿着一个形状像公鸡的饼干罐快步走了进来。他取下了饼干罐的盖子。

"要吃点饼干吗?"他问。

每个孩子拿了一块饼干。

斯皮韦茨先生在妻子身旁坐下。"好吧,"他说,"你们几个孩子想干什么?"

"我们在报纸上看到了这里闹鬼的消息。"露丝说。

"于是我们就来看一看。"丁丁说。

"但是,我们没看到鬼!"乔希补充道。

"然后林克莱特先生告诉我们,那只鬼正在摧毁酒店的生意。"露丝接着说,"于是我们决定对这件事进行调查!"

斯皮韦茨太太瞪大眼睛看着孩子们。"调查?"她问,"像侦探一样?"

"对。"丁丁回答完,问斯皮韦茨太太,"您看见鬼了吗?"

斯皮韦茨太太看向丈夫。"没有,但我们听到了。是吧,亲爱的?"

老先生点点头说:"连续两晚!墙壁里传来可怕的声音。有一个声音呼唤着我的名字!'埃比尼泽,'那声音说,'离开,离开!'"

乔希急忙吞下口中的食物,问:"它知道您的名字?"

"那个声音也对我说话了。"斯皮韦茨太太说,"它说:'弗洛,离开这个地方!'"

她哭了起来,边哭边拿着一块蕾丝手帕擦眼泪。

斯皮韦茨先生拍了拍妻子的手。"我们刚刚做了一个艰难的决定,"他对孩子们说,"我们要卖掉酒店。有家纽约的房地产公司想购买这家酒店。"

"卖掉香格里拉?!"丁丁脱口而出。

"不能卖!"露丝说。

"我们之前打算把酒店留给我们的侄子,"斯皮韦茨太太说，"但现在……"

"现在看来，酒店将归易奇、雷尔和鲁克所有。"斯皮韦茨先生说。

"他们是谁？"露丝问。

"他们是那家房地产公司的三个合伙人。"斯皮韦茨先生说，"这几个月他们一直追着我们，要我们卖酒店。"

他走到一张小桌子前，拿出一封信。"他们想拆掉香格里拉酒店，在这里建造一栋高层建筑！"他说。

斯皮韦茨先生将信放到茶盘上，说："我和我太太不想卖，但我们不知道还能怎么办。不知道为什么，我们总有一种辜负了酒店客人的感觉。"

他低头看着斯皮韦茨太太说："我今天给房地产公司打了电话，他们明天就会带着合同来找我们签字。"

斯皮韦茨太太抬起头，双眼通红。"我们还能做点什么吗？"她问。

斯皮韦茨先生握住太太的手，说："为了你，我愿意做任何事，但我太老了，打不了鬼了。"

"我们不老！"丁丁说着，跳了起来，"我们会找到那只鬼，然后除掉它！"他看向乔希和露丝，问："对吧，伙伴们？"

"对！"露丝说。

斯皮韦茨先生满面笑容。"你们被录用了！"他说。

乔希呻吟了一声。"我还能再要一块饼干吗？"他问。

第四章

"我们怎么把鬼除掉?"乔希在电梯里问,"就算我真的相信有鬼。"

"还不知道。"丁丁回答,"但我们不能让那些房地产商将香格里拉酒店拆了!"

电梯门开了,林克莱特先生正站在前台后面,眼神空洞茫然。

"去我家吧。"丁丁低声说,"我们可以边吃东西边计划一下。"

"好!"乔希说,"刚才的饼干太小了,跳蚤的肚子都填不饱!"

丁丁哈哈大笑起来。"不是每个人的肚子都像大峡谷那么大,乔希!"

他们沿着主街往北走,然后经过绿地小学外围的银环路回到丁丁家。

丁丁拿出花生酱和面包。乔希找到一袋椒盐脆饼干。露丝为大家倒了牛奶。

"我的三明治要多抹点花生酱。"乔希要求,"我都快饿晕了!"

丁丁把花生酱和面包向乔希推了过去:"我可不是您的仆人,殿下。"

乔希咧嘴笑了,开始制作三明治。

"好了。"丁丁在桌边坐下,"你们要怎么除鬼?"

"首先你得证明确实有鬼。"乔希说着,咬了一大口三明治。

"你还是不信酒店有鬼吗?"露丝问。

乔希将口中的食物吞下,摇着头说:"不信。"

A to Z 神秘案件

他在桌子上并排放了四块椒盐脆饼干。"我们问过莉薇,但她没有看见鬼。"乔希说完,拿起一块椒盐脆饼干吃了起来。

"然后我们问了林克莱特先生是否看见过鬼,但他说没见过。"乔希又吃了一块椒盐脆饼干。

接着,他拿起剩下的两块饼干,说:"斯皮韦茨先生和太太也没有看见鬼,他们只是听到了声音!"

乔希将那两块饼干也塞进了嘴里。"伙伴们,"他一边咀嚼一边说,"我们问过的人都没有看见鬼,因此也许根本没有鬼!"

丁丁和露丝盯着乔希。

"他说得对。"片刻后,露丝说,"我们问过的人都说是别人看见了鬼。"

"我们应该怎么做?"丁丁问。

"我们必须亲眼见一见那只鬼。"露丝说。

丁丁眨了眨眼睛。"但是,我们要怎么做呢?"他问。

乔希舔了舔手指上的花生酱。"呃，我们可以先去找真正看见过鬼的人。"

"但是看见过鬼的人都已经退房离开了。"露丝说。

丁丁一口吞下剩下的三明治。"我们必须和那些人谈谈。"他说，"也许林克莱特先生能帮助我们。"

"好主意。"露丝说，"我们再去一趟酒店吧。"

"没有甜点吗？"乔希问。

"擦掉你唇边的牛奶沫，然后出发！"丁丁说。

孩子们又急匆匆地回到酒店。他们进去时，林克莱特先生抬起头看向他们。"我听说你们和我的姑妈、姑父聊过了。"他说。

"他们雇用了我们，让我们帮忙除鬼！"丁丁告诉他。

林克莱特先生嘴角抽动，勉强扯出一个微笑，问："你们有计划了吗？"

"差不多。"露丝说，"但我们需要知道看见鬼的客人的姓名和电话号码。"

林克莱特先生摇着头说:"对不起,即使客人离开了,我们也必须保护他们的隐私。"

"那么,酒店里还有客人吗?"她问。

林克莱特先生指着在大堂角落里看书的一对男女说:"杰弗斯先生和太太还没有离开,但我不知道他们是否看见了鬼。"

"我们去问问他们!"丁丁说完,朝着他们走去。

男人身穿牛仔裤、登山靴和白色毛衣。

女人有着一头黑发,穿着深蓝色的毛衣和褪了色的牛仔裤。

"嘿,杰弗斯先生,杰弗斯太太。"丁丁说,"我叫丁丁,他们是我的朋友乔希和露丝。我们正在调查酒店闹鬼事件。你们看见鬼了吗?"

"你们为什么想知道?"男人问。

"因为酒店的主人雇我们除掉它!"露丝回答。

"要是真的有鬼的话。"乔希嘀咕道。

"真的有!"杰弗斯太太说,"把我吓了个半死!"

"所以你们看见了?"丁丁问。

酒店奇异事件

"我们都看见了。"杰弗斯放下书说,"昨晚,我们在这里打牌,一直打到午夜。正当我们上楼回房间时,那东西突然出现了!"

杰弗斯太太打了个寒战。"走廊里的空气仿佛突然就冷了下来!"她说。

"它长什么样子?"露丝问。

杰弗斯先生闭上眼睛回忆:"那只鬼走路时散发着幽幽的光芒,她一头乱糟糟的白色长发,身穿一件发光的长袍。"

"还有,眼睛的位置是两个黑洞!"杰弗斯太太补充道。

"您说'长发',"露丝说,"是女鬼吗?"

杰弗斯先生看向露丝,说:"嗯,我是这么认为的,至少那件长袍看起来像是女士穿的。"

"您还说那只鬼'走路',"丁丁说,"它有脚吗?"

"脚?"杰弗斯先生说,"我不能肯定,我们当时急着进房间。"

这时,林克莱特先生来到沙发前。"打扰一下,丁丁。"他说,"我姑父打电话找你。"

"斯皮韦茨先生想要和我通话?"丁丁问。

林克莱特先生点点头。丁丁跟着他去接电话。

"喂?"丁丁接起电话,听对方说了好几分钟,然后挂断电话,回到乔希和露丝身边。

"你们不会相信这是真的。"他说。

"别告诉我他们看见了那只鬼!"乔希说。

"不是,但也许我们能看见。"丁丁说,"斯皮韦茨先生想让我们今晚睡在酒店!"

第五章

乔希和露丝盯着丁丁。

"真的。"丁丁说。

"为什么啊?"露丝问。

"因为酒店基本空了,他说这么做是帮他的忙。"丁丁说,"如果人们看见我们住在这儿,他们可能会认为闹鬼只是个玩笑。"

"就住在这儿!"乔希说,"我需要离开双胞胎一晚！"

丁丁笑着说："斯皮韦茨先生也邀请了我们的家人，他想让我们住在这里调查闹鬼的事！"

乔希笑了起来。他说："我的弟弟们在这里的时候，那只鬼最好当心点！"

到了吃晚餐的时候，一切准备就绪。三家人将在香格里拉酒店度过这个夜晚。

露丝的小弟弟纳特很想认识那只鬼。

"它会是我的朋友！"纳特说，"我们可以一起玩恐龙！"

丁丁的家人是与露丝的家人共乘一辆车来的酒店。

孩子们到时，乔希家的车已经开进了停车场。乔希紧紧抱住他的两个弟弟——布赖恩和布拉德利。两个男孩抱着一对一模一样的泰迪熊。

锁好车后，他们三家，一共十二个人，走进了香格里拉酒店。斯皮韦茨先生和太太已经在大堂里等着他们了。他们盛装打扮，仿佛这是特别重要的场合。

"大家晚上好！"斯皮韦茨先生招呼道，"欢迎入住香格里拉!"

他们和几个大人握手。

"你们真是太周到了。"丁丁的妈妈对他们说。

斯皮韦茨太太朝孩子们微笑。"这没什么。这三位侦探今晚要去查酒店闹鬼的事!"

丁丁的父亲笑着说:"只要他们在睡觉时间前查就行!"

"爸爸!"丁丁说着,翻了个白眼。

这时,林克莱特先生也走了过来。"卡斯珀[1]在哪里?"纳特问他,"我想看看鬼!"

林克莱特先生朝纳特眨了眨眼,然后将房间钥匙递给丁丁、乔希和露丝。

"你们一定会喜欢你们的房间。"他说,"我为小朋友们准备了折叠床。"

丁丁带他们去乘电梯。

"你们的房间号是多少?"乔希问,"我的是203。"

"我的在走廊对面,"露丝说,"204。"

---

1. 卡斯珀:卡通形象,一个可爱的幽灵小鬼。——译者

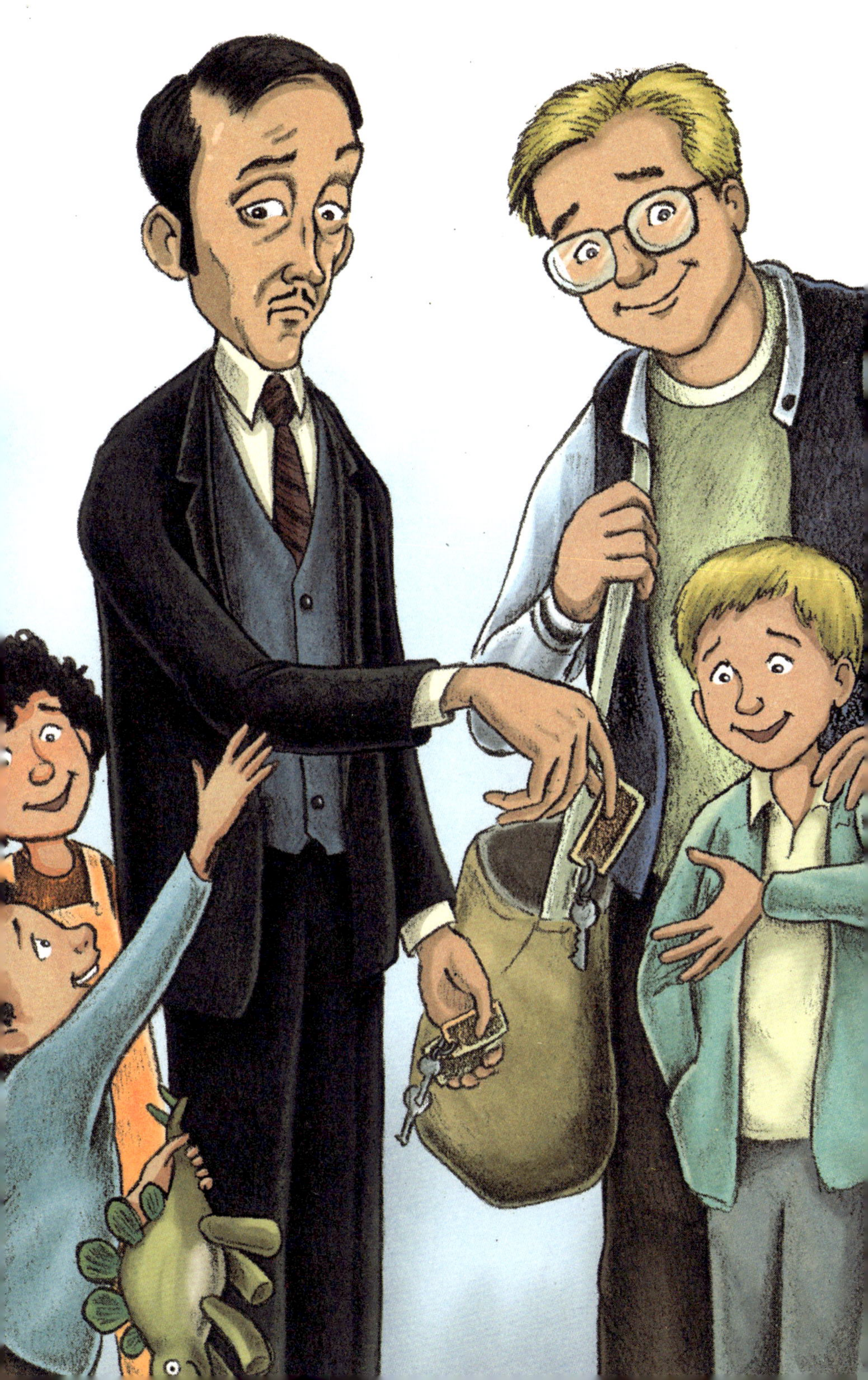

"我的也在走廊对面,"丁丁说,"202。"

五分钟后,三家人全都进了房间。丁丁把他的背包扔到一张窄窄的折叠床上。

房间很大,配有彩色电视机和小型冰箱。丁丁打开冰箱门,发现里面有一些软饮料[1]和零食。

"这些东西我们能吃吗?"丁丁问。

他父亲板起了脸:"你刚吃完晚餐,丁丁!"

丁丁笑着说:"是的,我知道。我最晚能几点睡?"

"九点。"他妈妈回答,"别忘了,明天是周一。"

"妈妈,明天是哥伦布日[2]!"丁丁说着,脸上堆满了笑容,"不用上学!"

"好吧,十点,一分钟都不能超!"

丁丁离开房间,敲响了乔希房间的门。"进来!"房间里传来其中一个双胞胎弟弟的叫声。

丁丁打开门,乔希家住的房间比他家住的还要大,大床对面的三张小床一字排开。

---

1. 软饮料:不含酒精的饮料,如汽水、果汁等。——编者
2. 哥伦布日:又称哥伦比亚日,时间是10月的第二个周一。——编者

布赖恩和布拉德利穿着款式相同的蝙蝠侠睡衣，正在填色图画书上涂着颜色。

乔希正站在小冰箱前吃花生。

"乔希可以出来玩吗？"丁丁满面笑容地问。

乔希的爸爸说："当然可以，只要在吃早餐前回来就行。"

乔希喜笑颜开。"我们去找露丝。"他对丁丁说。

他们走到204房间，敲了敲门。露丝打开门走了出来。"我父母正在哄纳特睡觉。"她小声说。

"我们去楼下大堂想一想接下来的计划吧。"丁丁提议。

"我已经有了计划！"露丝说。

"真的？"丁丁问。

露丝点点头。"林克莱特先生告诉我们那只鬼在午夜出现，对不对？杰弗斯先生和太太也这么说。"

乔希哼了一声，说："你的计划是什么？在时钟敲响十二下的时候，跑出去和鬼打招呼吗？"

露丝笑着回答："完全正确！"

第六章

"这里的气味太难闻了。"乔希咕哝道。

"乔希,这个柜子里装的是清洁用品,"丁丁对他说,"本来就不好闻。"

"你们两个就不能小声点?"露丝说,"你们想吵醒爸爸妈妈,让他们发现我们不在房间里吗?"

这时将近午夜十二点。十分钟前,三个孩子偷偷溜出房间,藏在了柜子里。

乔希打了个哈欠。"我本来应该正在睡觉，做美梦呢。"他说，"而现在，我却像沙丁鱼一样挤在这里，等着那只愚蠢的鬼出现，那只鬼甚至还不是真的存在！"

丁丁在黑暗中笑了。"我听说鬼讨厌红头发的小孩。"他悄声说。

"啊？哦，我还听说鬼把金发小孩当早餐！"

露丝突然伸出双手。"嘘，我好像听到了声音。"她说。

乔希哼了一声，说："干得好，露丝，但——"

"嘘！"丁丁悄声说，"我也听到了！"

他把柜门推开了一条缝，三个孩子全都目不转睛地盯着走廊。

丁丁听到了一声呻吟，就像风在山洞里的呜咽声。

突然，一个高大的白色身影出现在走廊尽头，泛着幽幽白光，仿佛飘浮在空中。

"天哪！"乔希惊呼，他的声音有些沙哑，"我想回床上睡觉！"

那只鬼穿着一件白色长袍，白色头发像尖刺

A to Z 神秘案件

一样根根竖起,本是眼睛的地方只有黑色的空洞。

乔希紧紧抓着丁丁的胳膊,把丁丁都弄疼了,但丁丁因为害怕,什么也说不出来。

白色身影慢慢地飘向孩子们的藏身之处,手里拿着一把银色的长剑。

"它知道我们在这里!"乔希声音沙哑。

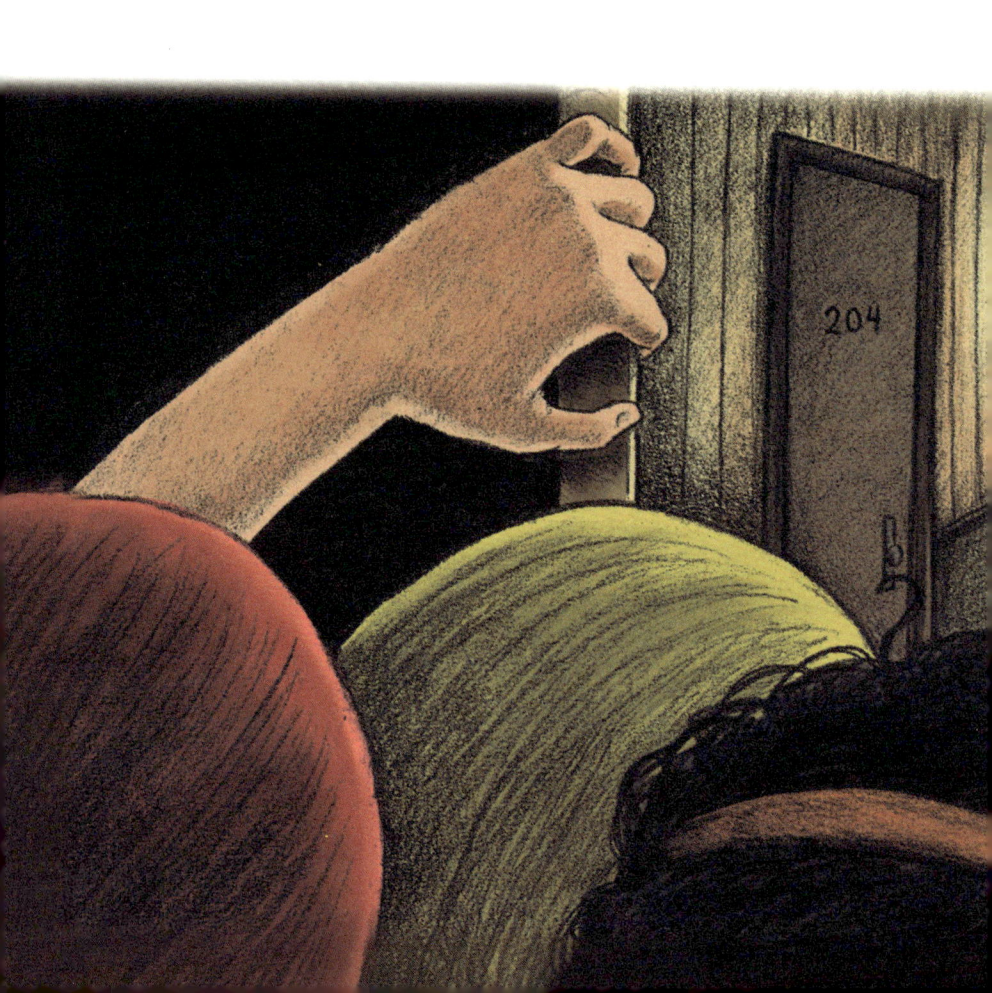

酒店奇异事件

那只鬼在每一扇门前停顿一下,最后停在了202房间的门前。

"那是我住的房间!"丁丁想。

"丁——丁——"那只鬼呻吟着,"回——家——这——个——地——方——危——险——"

丁丁的头发都竖了起来。他觉得浑身冰冷,仿佛有人打开了窗户似的。

那只鬼又飘到另一个房间门口。

这一次,它呻吟道:"乔——希——回家——赶——紧——离——开——"

在204房间的门外,那只鬼最后呻吟道:"露丝,带着你的家——人——速——速——离——开——"

然后,那只鬼便沿着来路飘走了。片刻后,走廊里又变得空无一人。

露丝跳了起来,将柜门推开。"快点,我们去看看它去了哪里!"她说。

"谁在乎它去了哪里!"乔希说,"我就待在这儿!"

"快点,乔希。"丁丁催促,"我答应了斯皮韦茨先生和太太,我们会把鬼除掉,我们只剩下现在到早上的时间了!"

"但是,它把我们除掉了怎么办?"

丁丁抓住乔希的胳膊,沿着走廊走去。他停下脚步,在202房间门口听了听。他听到了他爸爸的鼾声，于是笑了笑。

突然，乔希吸了吸鼻子，说："什么味道？"

丁丁耸耸肩，继续往前走。

露丝来到走廊尽头。"它消失了。"她对身旁的朋友们说。

"我在这里也闻到了。"乔希说。

"闻到了什么？"露丝问。

"不知道，"乔希说，"但它让我想起了什么。"

在拐角处，孩子们发现了一个灰色的金属门，门上贴着红色的"消防出口"标志。

"也许它是从这里离开的！"露丝指着那扇门小声说。

丁丁屏住呼吸，慢慢推开门。孩子们看向楼梯间，里面是通往楼上楼下的黑乎乎的台阶。

"我们是不是应该分头查看？"丁丁问。

"不行！"乔希说，"我们一起行动！"

丁丁笑着对乔希说："还认为闹鬼是开玩笑吗？"

乔希朝丁丁做了个鬼脸。

"伙伴们，"露丝说，"那只鬼怎么会知道我们的名字和我们住的房间号？"

"也许它有超自然力量!"乔希说。

"也许那只鬼真的是酒店里的人,"丁丁补充道,"认识我们的人!"

露丝点了点头说:"我认为那只鬼今晚出来只是为了找我们。"

"你的意思是,它只是想把我们吓跑,就像它之前吓跑其他人一样,对吗?"丁丁问。

露丝又点了点头。

"嗯,这招的确管用!"乔希说,"我们快点离开吧!"

"嘿,这是什么?"露丝从门框上扯下一根白头发,问道。

丁丁仔细检查了这根头发。"那只鬼就有这样的白头发。"他说。

"没错,"露丝说,"但鬼是不会掉头发的,只有人才会掉头发!"

突然,204房间的门开了,露丝的爸爸探出头来。他说:"好了,你们几个,该上床睡觉了。"

"但是,爸爸,我们刚……"露丝说。

她爸爸摇着头说:"现在就和你的朋友们说晚安,露丝。"

第七章

第二天早上九点,三家人下楼,来到大堂。露丝的父母在埃莉餐馆请大家吃了早餐,之后他们回酒店拿行李。

大人们向林克莱特先生和斯皮韦茨夫妇道谢时,孩子们挤到沙发上说话。

"我们接下来要怎么做?"丁丁问,"斯皮韦茨先生和太太今天就会卖掉酒店!"

露丝从口袋里掏出那根白头发。"这能证明那只鬼是人假扮的,"她说,"但是我们不知道那人是谁,为什么这么做。"

"也许这根白头发是哪个客人的。"乔希说。

"乔希,除了杰弗斯先生和太太,所有的客人都离开了,而他们俩都是黑头发。"露丝提醒道。

"这根头发是不是假发上的?"丁丁问,"那只鬼可能穿着道具服装,并且化了妆。"

"就是这样!"乔希大声说,"昨晚我在走廊里闻到了化妆品的味道。我还记得去年万圣节的难闻气味!"

这时,林克莱特先生向孩子们走了过来。他看上去比前一天更加难过。

"今天是悲伤的一天。"林克莱特说,"中午,易奇、雷尔和鲁克将会带着合同到达这里。"

"中午!"露丝跳了起来,"这样的话,我们还剩三个小时!"

林克莱特先生低头注视着她。"恐怕来不及了。"他说着,摇头走开了。

"我们必须找出是谁假扮的鬼。"露丝说,"如果我们找不出,莉薇和林克莱特先生都将失去工作!"

"斯皮韦茨先生和太太也会失去他们的家!"丁丁补充道。

"伙伴们,我好像知道那只鬼是谁了。"乔希说。

丁丁和露丝瞪大眼睛看着他。

"说吧,"丁丁说,"是谁?"

"酒店里剩下的人是莉薇,林克莱特先生和他的姑妈、姑父,对不对?"

"对。"露丝回答。

"我们知道,他们中没人愿意酒店被拆除。"乔希继续说。

"你忘了杰弗斯先生和太太。"丁丁说,"他们还在这里。"

乔希咧嘴笑了:"说对了!"

"杰弗斯先生和太太吗?"露丝说,"但他们说他们在房间外看见了那只鬼。"

"他们的确看见了鬼,"乔希说,"因为他们中的一个就是鬼!"

"我知道怎么证明这一点。"丁丁说,"我们去搜查他们的房间。"

"林克莱特先生绝对不会允许我们这么做。"乔希说。

"嗯,也许他不会允许,但我知道有人可能会。"露丝说。

"谁?"丁丁问。

"莉薇!"

孩子们和他们的家人说完再见,就急忙朝着通往地下室的门走去。

他们发现莉薇正在一个舒适的房间里喝茶,她身上穿着服务员的工作服。"上午好,孩子们。"她向孩子们打招呼,"你们怎么来这里了?"

"我们昨晚看见那只鬼了!"露丝说。

莉薇瞪大了眼睛:"真的?在哪儿?快告诉我!"

孩子们向她讲述了他们昨晚在酒店过夜,以及躲在清洁柜里的事。

"太可怕了!"乔希说,"我们先是听到了奇怪的声音,然后这东西就凭空冒了出来!"

"它发着光!"露丝说着,给莉薇看了那根白头发,"我们还发现了这个!"

"我们认为那只鬼是某个客人穿着道具服装、戴着假发假扮的。"丁丁说。

莉薇瞬间惊呼:"那是假发!"

"什么?"露丝问。

"我刚想起,"莉薇说,"昨天我准备用吸尘器打扫301房间。在整理床下的鞋子和其他东西时,我看到一个毛茸茸的白色物件。我还以为是只老鼠,但那可能就是一顶白色的假发!"

"谁住在301房间?"丁丁问。

莉薇耸了耸肩。"我不知道他们的姓名,但他们是一对来自纽约的相当不错的夫妇。"

"你能放我们进房间找找线索吗?"露丝问。

莉薇摇着头说:"不行,你们很清楚,林克莱特先生非常重视保护客人的隐私。"

"但是斯皮韦茨先生和太太雇了我们除鬼!"丁丁说,"而且,如果他们必须卖掉酒店,你和林克莱特先生都将失去工作!"

"斯皮韦茨先生和太太也将搬走。"露丝补充道,"求你了,莉薇,我们不需要多长时间。"

酒店奇异事件

　　莉薇想了一会儿。"好吧。"最后她说,"但就两分钟!"

　　"咦,这是什么?"乔希将头伸进墙上的一个小口子。

　　"那是个老旧的小型升降机。"莉薇解释道,"过去,酒店会把食物给客人送上去。每个房间都有这么一个小型升降机,食物被送上去后,客人只要打开一扇门,就可以将托盘拿出来。"

　　"我们的房间没有。"丁丁说。

　　"其他房间也没有了。"莉薇说,"酒店在关

掉厨房后，小型升降机的口子便被封住了。"

她指着她墙上的口子说："那是仅剩的一个。"

乔希将头伸了进去："真酷！这里可以通往上面！"

"没错。"莉薇解释道，"升降机井还在，但通往房间的口子被封住了。"

乔希对着空井大声喊"喂！"，他的声音反射了回来。

莉薇喝完了茶。"好吧，我们现在就去。"她说，"要是林克莱特先生能恢复正常状态，我会很高兴的。现在的他和平时相比，脾气更加不好！"

莉薇带着孩子们上到三楼，敲了敲301房间的门，没人应门。于是莉薇用钥匙开了门锁，把门推开。

"请不要碰任何东西。"她说着，趴到地上，看了看两张床的下面，"假发不见了！"

孩子们四下查看着房间。"也许在柜子里！"露丝低声说。

莉薇拉开柜门。柜子最上面一层放着一个塑料的假人头，假人头上戴着有如尖刺般的白色假发。

"就是这个！"乔希说。

酒店奇异事件

"可以拿下来吗?"丁丁问。

莉薇小心翼翼地拿下塑料的假人头,放到桌子上。

露丝从口袋里掏出那根白发,拿着它凑近了假发。

"一样的头发!"她说。

第八章

"看!"丁丁指着床头柜上的一个小相框说,"杰弗斯先生和太太!"

"你们认识他们?"莉薇问。

"我们昨天见过他们。"露丝说,"我们认为装鬼的就是他们中的一个。"

莉薇的眼睛瞪得大大的。"他们为什么要吓

跑客人？他们看上去都是好人！"

"这正是我们要弄清楚的问题。"丁丁说。

莉薇小心翼翼地将假发放回柜子的层板上。

她后退时，胳膊碰到了什么东西。一个长长的银色物件"当啷"一声掉到了地板上。

"是那只鬼的剑！"露丝说着，捡起剑，笑出声来，"只是上了颜色的木头！"

"伙伴们，看这些东西！"乔希正仔细查看着梳妆台上的瓶瓶罐罐，"看，白色的小丑化妆的东西。还有黑色的！我昨天夜里在走廊里闻到的就是这个！"

"嘿，伙伴们，盒式录音机。"露丝说。

"孩子们，请别碰……"

莉薇话还没说完，露丝就按下了播放按钮。

房间里顿时响起诡异的声音。莉薇和孩子们听到一个声音在呻吟、呜咽。

"这声音和我们昨夜听到的一样！"丁丁说。

"你今天早上看见杰弗斯先生和太太了吗？"露丝问莉薇。

莉薇摇头。"也许他们出去吃早餐了。"她看

了一下表,说道,"我得去忙了。"

他们出来后,莉薇锁上了房门,然后他们全都进了电梯。

"谢谢你让我们进去。"露丝对莉薇说。

莉薇在唇间竖起一根手指。"这件事要保密,知道吗?"她悄声说,"不要告诉任何人!"

"一言为定。"露丝也悄声说。

电梯门开了,莉薇离开了,孩子们则留在了大堂里。

"林克莱特先生在那儿。"乔希说,"也许他知道杰弗斯先生和太太去了哪里。"

孩子们向前台走去。

林克莱特先生看上去一夜没睡。他的西装皱巴巴的,他后面的头发翘了起来。

"也许我们不该打搅他。"露丝低声说。

"但是我们必须找到杰弗斯先生和太太,"丁丁说,"我们没有很多时间了!"

丁丁走到前台,露出一个最可爱的笑容,对

他打招呼:"嘿,林克莱特先生!"

林克莱特先生低头看着丁丁。"哦,你好。"他说。

"请问您知道杰弗斯先生和太太去了哪里吗?"他问。

林克莱特先生朝着大门抬了抬手说,"他们告诉我,他们要去埃莉餐馆吃早餐。"

"谢谢,林克莱特先生!"丁丁说。

孩子们离开了酒店,匆匆沿着主街往埃莉餐馆走去。

"我们要怎么和他们说呢?"乔希问,"我们总不能走上前去,谴责他们装神弄鬼吧?"

露丝推开餐馆的门。"别担心,"她说,"我有一个计划。"

埃莉站在柜台后面,搅拌着一个大碗里的金枪鱼沙拉。孩子们坐到了一个卡座里,她朝他们挥了挥手。

"他们在那里。"乔希低声说道,朝着另一个卡座的方向点了下头。杰弗斯先生和太太正在那里吃早餐。

"他们看上去像好人,"丁丁说,"不像是想毁掉酒店的人。"

埃莉来到他们所在的卡座。"这么快就回来了?"她问着,翻开点单的本子,"不要告诉我,你们还想再吃一顿早餐!"

"我们能借用一下你的本子和铅笔吗?"露丝问。

埃莉向露丝露出一个会心的微笑,将本子和铅笔递给她。"你们几个要干什么?"她问。

"一会儿还您。"露丝说。

"好的,那我一会儿再过来。"埃莉说完,就回去继续搅拌金枪鱼沙拉了。

露丝动笔写了起来。

"你这是干什么?"乔希问。

"等一下!"露丝说道。写完后,她把本子推到丁丁和乔希跟前,问他们:"你们觉得怎么样?"

"露丝!要是我们弄错了,不是杰弗斯先生他们怎么办?"丁丁问。

"我们不会错。"露丝说完,站起身。

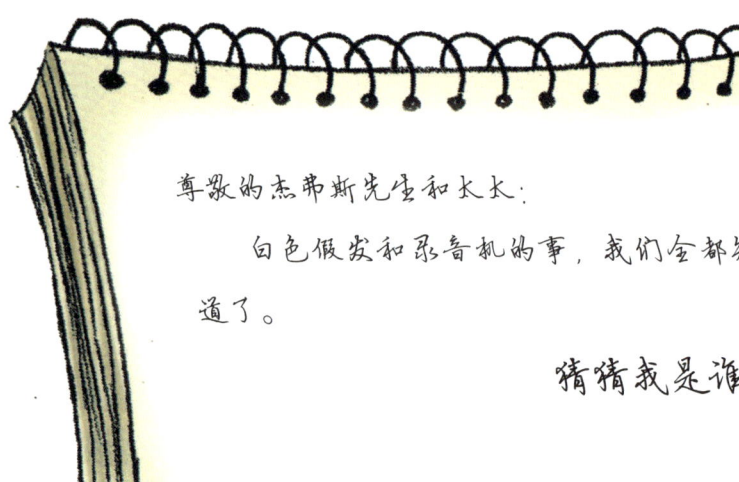

A to Z 神秘案件

> 尊敬的杰弗斯先生和太太:
>
> 　　白色假发和录音机的事，我们全都知道了。
>
> 　　　　　　　　猜猜我是谁！

　　她走到埃莉跟前，和她说了什么，把本子递给她。埃莉朝露丝笑了笑，然后向杰弗斯夫妇的卡座走去。

　　露丝匆匆回来坐下。"现在好好看着。"她告诉丁丁和乔希。

　　他们看着埃莉将纸条交给杰弗斯太太。

　　杰弗斯太太看了纸条后，对埃莉说了什么，埃莉指了指孩子们。

　　杰弗斯太太朝他们挥了挥手，露丝也挥手回应。

　　"走吧。"露丝说着，朝杰弗斯夫妇的卡座走去，丁丁和乔希紧跟在她身后。

"嘿！"露丝打完招呼，从口袋里掏出那根白头发，"我想昨天夜里您的假发刮到了消防门上。您留下了这个。"

她将白头发放在绿色的餐垫上。

杰弗斯太太瞪大眼睛看着头发，然后看向孩子们，最后看向了她的丈夫。

杰弗斯先生叹了一口气，笑着对孩子们说："看来被你们识破了！"

第九章

"那只鬼真的是你们扮的吗?"露丝问。

杰弗斯先生点头。"昨夜是我扮的,"他说,"之前的两个夜晚是辛迪。"

他看着孩子们说:"昨夜我出来的时候,你们没有在房间里睡觉吗?"

"我们躲在一个气味难闻的柜子里,看见了

你!"乔希说。

杰弗斯先生笑了。"我扮得像吗?"

"您确实吓到我了!"乔希说。

"但是,你们为什么要这么做呢?"露丝问。

"我们两个都是演员,但是我们破产了。"杰弗斯太太说,"几周前,有三个人在一次彩排后找上我们,问我们想不想要一份工作。"

"我们告诉他们,我们当然想要!"杰弗斯先生说,"那三个人让我们入住香格里拉酒店,把客人吓走。我们自己设计了鬼的道具服装。"

"你们是怎么让服装发光的?"乔希问。

"我在长袍里粘了一串小灯泡,"杰弗斯太太说,"电池安在假发下面。"

杰弗斯先生微笑着说:"我想到可以将录音机藏在升降机井的地下室,录音机发出的声音就能沿着酒店墙壁传出去!"

"但是这样做实在是太卑鄙了!"露丝说,"要是酒店关门,林克莱特先生、莉薇、斯皮韦茨先生和太太会怎么样呢?"

杰弗斯先生举起双手。"谁说酒店要关门?"

"斯皮韦茨先生和太太说的。"丁丁说,"他们因为你们的装神弄鬼要卖掉酒店!"

"什么?"杰弗斯太太说,"斯皮韦茨先生和太太应该知道闹鬼的事啊,林克莱特先生应该也知道。"

"听我说,"杰弗斯先生说,"雇用我们的那三个人告诉我们,酒店将会用于拍摄恐怖电影,装鬼把客人吓跑应该能起到很好的宣传效果。所有客人都能得到全额退款,还可以获得免费的电影票。"

"我们会在电影中担任主演!"杰弗斯太太说,"这对我们来说将是一个很大的突破!"

孩子们面面相觑。

"但是斯皮韦茨先生和太太根本不知道电影的事,"露丝说,"林克莱特先生也不知道。他们真的很难过,因为他们只能卖掉酒店,就在今天!"

"没错,"乔希说,"斯皮韦茨太太都难过得哭了!"

"我们甚至见到了房地产公司寄来的那封信。"丁丁说,"名字好像是什么皮奇或鲁奇。"

酒店奇异事件

"易奇、雷尔和鲁克?"杰弗斯先生突然开口。

"是的!"丁丁说。"他们一直想买下这家酒店,但斯皮韦茨先生拒绝了他们——直到现在。"

杰弗斯先生看向他的妻子。"噢,不!"他说,"雇用我们的正是易奇、雷尔和鲁克!"

杰弗斯太太原本很开心,现在却难过起来。她说:"难怪他们让我们不要和林克莱特先生提起拍电影的事。原来根本就没有这回事!"

杰弗斯太太摇着头说:"他们想要的是酒店,而我们成了帮凶!"

"我感到很难过。"杰弗斯太太说着,看向她的丈夫,"托德,我们有什么办法弥补犯下的过错吗?"

杰弗斯先生看着孩子们。"你们觉得现在还来得及吗?"他问,"他们真的已经卖掉酒店了吗?"

丁丁扫了一眼柜台上方的挂钟。"他们计划中午签合同。"他说,"但我想,我知道你们怎么做可以摆脱易奇、雷尔和鲁克,同时又能挽救酒店!"

第十章

"这假发让人头皮发痒!"乔希抱怨道。他、丁丁和露丝正躲在酒店大堂的前台后面。

乔希打扮成鬼,戴着假发,穿着长袍,还化了妆。

"不用等很久了。"丁丁说着,瞥了一眼挂钟。马上到中午了!

"易奇、雷尔和鲁克最好能快点。"乔希说,"我就要因为这件愚蠢的衣服窒息而死了!"

从他们藏身的地方,丁丁可以看到整个大堂。林克莱特先生和他的姑妈、姑父坐在沙发上。

在大堂的另一边,杰弗斯先生和太太正与《绿地报》的记者琳达·戈麦斯玩牌。她的边上坐着一个拿着照相机的男人。

"他们要是不来怎么办?"露丝悄声问。

丁丁露出微笑,指着前门说:"我想他们已经来了!"

三个男人走进酒店大堂。一个高个子,一个中等个子,一个又矮又胖。他们都穿着黑西装、白衬衣,打着蓝色领带。

"他们看上去像三只企鹅!"乔希说。

林克莱特先生急忙朝那三个人迎了上去,然后领着他们回到他姑妈和姑父跟前。

高个子男人与斯皮韦茨先生握了握手。"我是弗莱彻·易奇。"他说。

"我是伦道夫·雷尔。"中等个子的男人说着,伸出了手。

"我是迈尔斯·鲁克。"矮个子的男人说着,与斯皮韦茨先生握了握手。

斯皮韦茨先生朝三个人点了点头。"合同带来了吗?"他问。

弗莱彻·易奇满面笑容地说:"当然带来了!"他递给斯皮韦茨先生一份看起来很重要的文件。

伦道夫·雷尔从公文包里取出一个信封,说:"这是支票。"

迈尔斯·鲁克迅速从口袋里掏出一支金笔,说:"您只需要签名即可,斯皮韦茨先生。"

斯皮韦茨先生伤心地看向他的妻子,然后接过笔,准备在文件上签名。

就在这时,杰弗斯先生和太太走了过来。

"看,托德!"杰弗斯太太说,"电影制片人!"

"真巧!"杰弗斯先生说,"我们刚刚还在谈论你们将在酒店拍摄的电影!"

斯皮韦茨先生顿了顿。"什么电影?"他狐疑地问。

"嗯……"弗莱彻·易奇犹豫着。

"呃……"伦道夫·雷尔也不知道怎么开口。

"我……我们可以解释!"迈尔斯·鲁克说。

"没有必要解释,"琳达·戈麦斯说着,站了起来,走向这三个人,"我是《绿地报》的记者。我将在明天的专栏告诉全镇居民,你们是如何耍诡计,试图通过欺骗让酒店主人卖掉酒店的!"

这三个人瞪着眼睛看向琳达,然后看向杰弗斯夫妇。最后,他们的视线落在了斯皮韦茨先生和太太身上。

弗莱彻·易奇脸红了。

伦道夫·雷尔脸色惨白。

迈尔斯·鲁克的脸则涨成了紫红色。香格里

酒店奇异事件

拉酒店大堂一时陷入死一般的寂静。

突然,一只戴着白色假发的鬼从前台后方飘了过来,它的头发如尖刺般根根竖起。"回家——"它发出令人毛骨悚然的呻吟声,"赶紧——回家——"

除了易奇、雷尔和鲁克,大堂里的人都哈哈大笑起来。

"我想我不需要这个了。"斯皮韦茨先生说着,将手中的文件撕成碎片。

"你……你在做什么?!"弗莱彻·易奇气急败坏地说。

"你不能中途退出与易奇、雷尔和鲁克的交易!"迈尔斯·鲁克说。

"你们已经同意卖掉酒店了!"伦道夫·雷尔说。

斯皮韦茨太太站到了丈夫身边。"你们叫易奇、雷尔和鲁克?"她说,"你们真应该把名字改为坑、蒙、骗![1]"

---

1. 三人原名为"Eatch, Rail, and Roock",字母重新排列组合为"Cheat, Liar, and Crook",意思为坑、蒙、骗。——译者

"现在,"斯皮韦茨先生说,"我想你们该离开了。"

林克莱特先生二话不说,把三人送出了大门。

带着相机的人跟在他们后面,拍了一张又一张照片。

所有人都欢呼起来,斯皮韦茨太太的欢呼声最为响亮。

杰弗斯太太回头对斯皮韦茨老夫妇说:"我和我丈夫为我们的行为感到非常抱歉,请问您二位

能原谅我们吗?"

"当然。"斯皮韦茨太太说。

"事实上,"斯皮韦茨先生说,"你们扮鬼扮得非常成功,我们想邀请你们继续扮下去!我们希望,你们每个月抽一个周末,为我们的客人上演一次'香格里拉谜案'。你们觉得怎么样?"

"这主意不错。"杰弗斯先生说,"我们还可以找一些演员朋友来帮忙!"

摄影师拍摄了杰弗斯夫妇和斯皮韦茨夫妇的照片。

"我们的读者看到这条消息时,一定会很震惊!"琳达·戈麦斯说着,在她的记事本上写下了这一切。

斯皮韦茨先生看向丁丁、乔希和露丝,说:"谈起谜案,我要感谢我们的三位超级大侦探!"

他从口袋里掏出三个信封。"我和斯皮韦茨太太衷心地感谢你们,"他说着,将信封递给孩子们,"请睡前再打开。"

孩子们的脸红了,此时,摄影师抓拍了一张照片。

"请一定要在你的专栏中提到他们的名字。"斯皮韦茨太太对琳达·戈麦斯说。

"乐意至极。"琳达说,"现在,让我们拍几张孩子们的照片吧,好吗?"

丁丁和露丝看向照相机,露出了微笑。

"等等！"乔希叫着，努力脱着扮鬼的服装，"我可不想自己戴着这顶假发、穿着这套衣服的照片出现在报纸上！"

那天晚上，孩子们聚在丁丁家的客厅里。

丁丁将洛蕾塔放在膝上。它正在啃他的一粒衬衫纽扣。

乔希拿出斯皮韦茨先生给他的信封。"我们现在能打开了吗？"他问。

"他说让我们睡前再打开，乔希。"丁丁说。

"现在就是我们的睡前时间！"

"乔希说得对！"露丝说，"我也很想知道我的信封里装了什么。我们数三个数，一起打开信封好吗？一、二、三！"

"噢，天哪！"乔希惊呼，"三张飞往佛罗里达的机票！"

露丝举起她信封里的东西，说："还有三张迪士尼乐园的门票！"

丁丁看到信封里的东西时，倒吸了一口气。他掏出三张五十美元的钞票和一张字条。字条上写着：

> 感谢你们挽救了我们的酒店，再次帮我们解决了一件香格里拉谜案！代我们向米老鼠与高飞问好！
>
> 衷心感谢你们的
> 斯皮韦茨夫妇

丁丁、乔希和露丝高兴得跳了起来，三人击掌庆贺。

洛蕾塔爬下沙发，看到没人注意它，开始啃咬起一张五十美元的钞票。

酒店奇异事件

A to Z Mysteries®

The Haunted Hotel

by **Ron Roy**

illustrated by
John Steven Gurney

INDIAN RIVER
LAWRENCE TAXI
RIVER ROAD
HORSE TRAILS
HORSES FOR RENT
BIKE PATH
WOODS
BIKE PATH
WOODVIEW ROAD
INDIAN WAY ROAD
FIRE STATION
BILL'S BIKES
SUPER MARKET
BRIDGE LANE
ROBIN ROAD
CROW ST
FINCH LA
THRUSH CT
OWL RD
PHEASANT LA
BLUE JAY WAY
WREN DR
FITNESS CENTER
WOODS
BIKE PATH
BLUE BIRD WAY
HUMMINGBIRD LA
WOODCOCK CROSS
ELLIE'S DINER
ACORN APTS
FURRY FEET PET SHOP
OAK STREET
CENTER CHURCH
BIKE PATH
PEOPLE'S POND
POST OFFICE
COMMUNITY GARDEN AND FISH POND
GREEN LAWN SAVINGS BANK
GOOSE ISLAND
POLICE STATION
ELDERLY HOUSING
RIVER ROAD
WEST GREEN ST
SENIOR COMMUNITY CENTER
GREEN LAWN LIBRARY
TOWN HALL
MAIN STREET
BIKE PATH
CHILDREN'S PETTING ZOO AND AQUARIUM
SHANGRI-LA HOTEL

WELCOME TO
GREEN LAWN
HOME OF THE
A to Z Mysteries
N
S
W
E
RIVER ROAD
BOAT LAUNCH
BOAT RENTAL
RON'S BAIT
DUCK WALK WAY
GREEN LAWN MIDDLE SCHOOL
EAGLE LANE
FARM LANE
JOSH
SQUAW ISLAND
GREEN LAWN ELEMENTARY SCHOOL
DINK
RUTH ROSE
TREE TOP CIRCLE
MEADOW ROAD
FOX LANE
QUAIL RUN ROAD
SILVER CIRCLE
WOODY STREET
BAND SHELL
ROSE GARDEN
PLEASANT STREET
THISTLE COURT
WILDFLOWER WAY
ROSE STREET
CENTER PARK
SWAN POND
GREEN LAWN HIGH SCHOOL
PLAYING FIELDS
GYM + POOL
BOXWOOD LANE
HOWARD'S BARBER-SHOP
BOOK NOOK
GAS STATION
CRYSTAL POND
MYSTIC GREENHOUSE
DOG KENNEL + VETERINARIAN
RIVER ROAD
EAST GREEN STREET
TOWN TENNIS COURTS
TOWN SWIMMING POOL
KIDDIE POOL
TOWN BASEBALL FIELD
TO THE BLUE HILLS

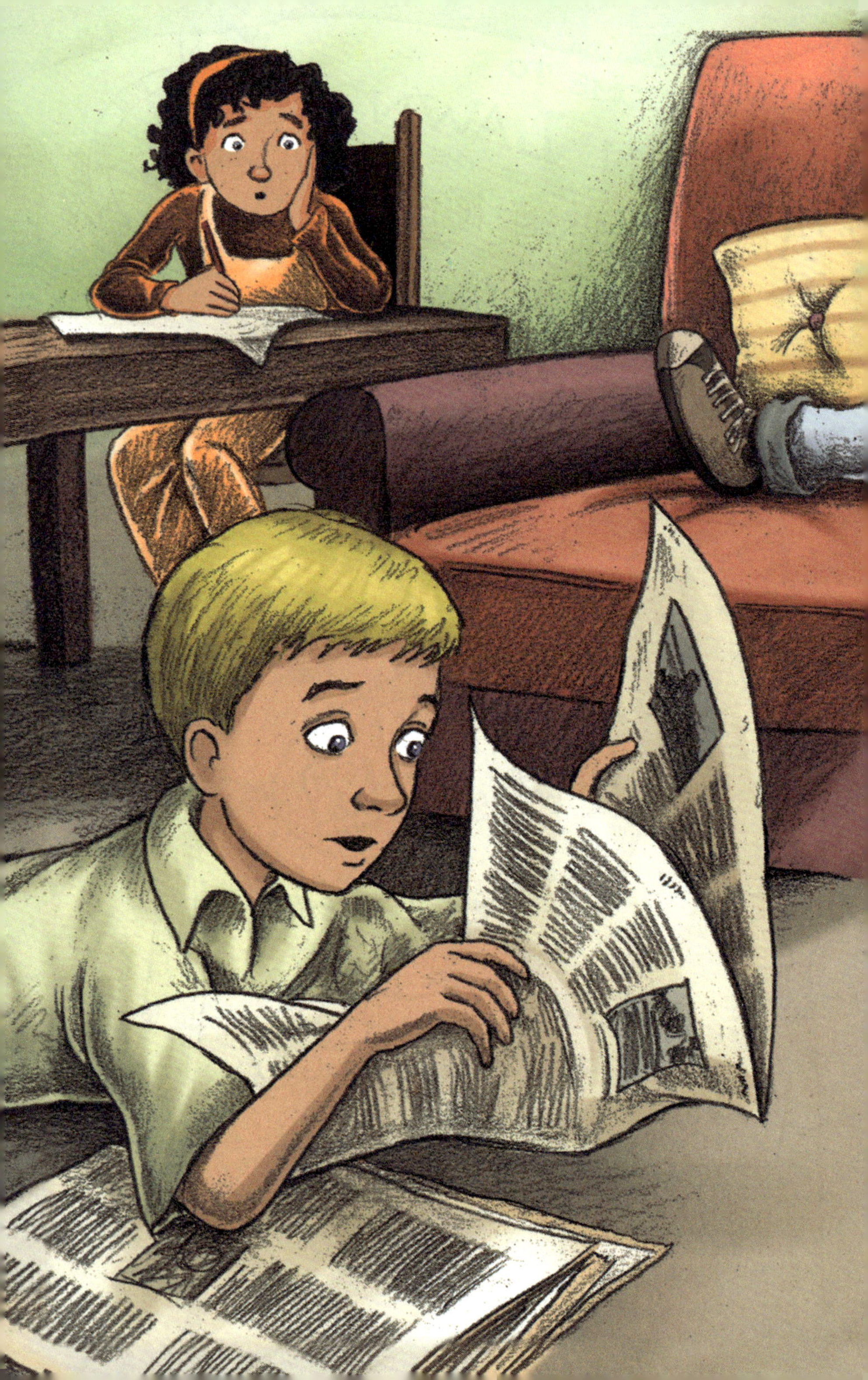

Chapter 1

"Oh my gosh!" Dink cried. "There's a ghost in Green Lawn!"

Donald David Duncan, Dink to his friends, was reading the Sunday newspaper on his living room floor.

Josh was sprawled on the sofa. He was using

raisins to teach Dink's guinea pig, Loretta, to do math.

Loretta gobbled up one of the raisins.

"Loretta!" Josh scolded. "If you keep eating all the raisins, you'll never learn to add!"

Ruth Rose was doing the crossword puzzle. "Maybe she's trying to teach you to subtract, Joshua," she said.

Josh tossed a raisin at her.

"I'm serious, you guys!" Dink said. He poked his finger at the *Green Lawn Gazette's* front page. "C'mere and read this!"

Ruth Rose glanced at the newspaper. "HEY, THAT'S MR. LINKLETTER!" she yelled.

Josh put Loretta in her cage, then read the headline over Dink's shoulder.

HAUNTED HOTEL! GHOST SCARES AWAY SHANGRI-LA GUESTS

"See, I told you," Dink said.

Josh grinned. "You don't really believe that stuff, do you?" he asked. "I'll bet it's a Halloween joke or something."

"Yeah, well, Mr. Linkletter looks pretty unhappy in this picture," Dink said. "And he never tells jokes!"

"Besides, Halloween isn't for two more weeks," Ruth Rose added.

Josh snorted. "Well, I don't believe in ghosts," he said. "Not until I see one with my own eyes!"

"Listen to this," Dink said, reading from the paper. " 'Guests report seeing a ghost floating down the hall at midnight. It was carrying a silver sword!' "

Josh snorted again. "Ghosts don't carry swords," he said.

Ruth Rose reached for her jacket. "Why don't we go to the hotel and see for ourselves?"

"Great idea," Dink said, pulling on his sneakers.

Josh let out a big sigh. "Okay, but I'm only coming to prove that I'm right."

The kids left Dink's house and headed around Silver Circle.

A bunch of kids were playing soccer at the elementary school. Their noses were pink and Dink could see their breath. The trees surrounding the playing field had turned red and gold.

On Main Street, a long banner hung between two telephone poles. Big letters spelled out the words: GREEN LAWN WELCOMES YOU TO FALL FOLIAGE WEEK, OCTOBER 13-20. COME SEE OUR COLORS!

The kids stopped across the street from the Shangri-la Hotel.

"Look!" Dink said.

People lugging suitcases were streaming out of the hotel:One woman was still wearing her slippers! They were pink and fluffy, with floppy bunny ears.

A newspaper reporter was trying to interview people as they left the hotel.

"Hello, sir," she said to one man. "I'm Linda Gomez from the *Green Lawn Gazette*. What's your reaction to the hotel ghost?"

"No comment!" the man snapped, and hurried away.

"Let's get her to interview us," Josh whispered. "Maybe we'll get our names in the paper!"

"We don't know anything yet," Dink said. "Come

on, let's find Mr. Linkletter."

The kids crossed the street and squeezed through the crowded doorway. Inside, Mr. Linkletter was standing behind the front desk, listening to a man and woman.

"...and we demand our money back!" the woman was saying. "We came here to see autumn leaves, not to be frightened by ghosts!"

Mr. Linkletter sighed. Dink noticed that his hair was mussed and his eyes were red.

"Of course, Mrs. Caruthers," he said. "You'll get a refund for the entire week. I'm sorry for this trouble. We've never had ghosts at the Shangri-la!"

Dragging their suitcases, the couple hurried past the kids and shoved through the doors.

"Boy, they looked mad," Josh said.

"Let's go talk to Mr. Linkletter," Dink said.

Just then the phone rang. Mr. Linkletter turned to answer it.

"Wait, there's Livvy," Ruth Rose said. "I wonder if

she knows anything."

Livvy Nugent was vacuuming the carpet near the elevators. She wore a white uniform with a dark blue apron.

"Hi, Livvy!" Ruth Rose said.

Livvy smiled and switched off the vacuum. "Ruth Rose! The last time I saw you, there was a kidnapping at the hotel. Now we've got a ghost!"

"We read about it in the newspaper," Ruth Rose said. "Is it true?"

"The guests sure think so!" Livvy said. "This place has been a madhouse since Friday night. Our biggest week of the year, and the guests are running out the door!"

Josh smirked. "Does the ghost jump out and say 'boo'?" he asked.

"Josh doesn't believe in ghosts," Ruth Rose said.

"Do you?" Livvy asked her.

Ruth Rose shrugged. "I don't know, but something's scaring the people away."

"Did you see the ghost?" Dink asked.

Livvy shook her head. "No, and I'd better not. When ghosts show up, I'm out of here!"

Just then Mr. Linkletter hung up the phone and walked over. "Ms. Nugent, please continue with your work," he said to Livvy.

Then he turned to the kids. "What can I do for you, children?"

"We read about the ghost," Dink said.

Josh rolled his eyes.

"And we saw all the people leaving," Ruth Rose said.

Mr. Linkletter's sad eyes surveyed the lobby. All the guests had left, and the place was empty.

Mr. Linkletter sighed. "Apparently a ghost is scaring away our guests," he said.

"Maybe we can help," Dink said. "Remember how we found Wallis Wallace when you thought she was kidnapped?"

"I'll never forget," Mr. Linkletter said. He looked at the three kids. His thin mustache twitched. His sad eyes squinted.

Finally he said, "Follow me, please." He turned and marched away.

Chapter 2

Mr. Linkletter led the kids to his office. The room was small, with just a desk and three chairs. On one wall hung a painting of the hotel. A framed picture of an elderly couple stood on the desk.

"Please sit down," Mr. Linkletter said.

The kids sat. Mr. Linkletter opened a desk drawer and took out a paper bag.

"Mint?" he asked.

Each of the kids took a mint from the bag and popped it into their mouths.

Mr. Linkletter looked inside the bag, then popped a mint into his mouth, too.

He sank back into his chair. "This is terrible," he said.

"Mine tastes okay," Josh said. "I think it's lemon."

Ruth Rose nudged Josh. "I think he means the ghost," she said.

Josh blushed. "Oh, sorry."

"As I was saying," Mr. Linkletter went on, "it all started two days ago, on Friday. It was almost midnight. I was closing my office when a guest ran into the lobby. She was yelling about a ghost on the third floor!"

"Did she say what the ghost looked like?" Dink asked.

Mr. Linkletter smoothed his hair. "She said it was all white—except for the black holes where its eyes should have been!"

The three kids looked at each other. Josh's mouth was hanging open.

Mr. Linkletter rubbed his temples as if he had a headache. "Anyway," he went on, "that guest checked out. Last night, more guests saw the ghost. Again, it appeared at midnight. Today, all those guests checked out."

Mr. Linkletter shook his head. "This ghost is ruining our business!"

"Did any of the guests say where the ghost went after they saw it?" Ruth Rose asked.

"Apparently it just floats away and disappears," he answered.

"Did you see the ghost, too?" Dink asked.

"No. I went upstairs, but all I saw was a dozen terrified guests!"

Mr. Linkletter picked up the picture of the elderly couple on his desk. "This is my aunt and uncle, Florence and Ebenezer Spivets. They've owned the Shangri-la ever since they were first married, forty-seven years ago."

He looked at the kids. "They're very worried. I don't know what will happen to the hotel if this ghost business continues …"

For a minute, nobody said anything. Finally Mr. Linkletter stood up.

"Now, if you'll excuse me," he said, "I have to tell my aunt and uncle that the Shangri-la Hotel won't be having a foliage week this year."

The kids thanked Mr. Linkletter and headed back out into the lobby.

A to Z 神秘案件

"Guys, we've gotta do something!" Dink whispered.

"But what can we do?" Ruth Rose asked.

Just then Livvy hurried over to them. "What'd he say?" she asked.

"He told us about the ghost," Ruth Rose said. She described it for Livvy.

"So there really is a ghost in the hotel!" Livvy said. She looked nervously over her shoulder. "What's Mr. Linkletter gonna do?"

"I don't know," Dink answered. He looked at Josh and Ruth Rose. "But we're gonna try to help, right?"

"Good luck!" Livvy said. "I'll be down in my cubbyhole eating lunch."

She opened a small door next to the elevator and disappeared.

"How're we s'posed to help?" Josh asked Dink. "We don't know anything about ghosts!"

"Well, I know one thing," Dink said. "No ghost is shutting down the Shangri-la if I have anything to do with it!"

"Dink is right," Ruth Rose said. "Mr. Linkletter is

our friend. We have to think of something!"

Suddenly the elevator door opened. A figure in white stood staring out at them.

"It's the ghost!" Josh screamed.

Chapter 3

The three kids stood frozen as the elevator door slid shut again.

For a minute, no one moved. Then Ruth Rose reached over and punched the up button for the elevator.

"What're you doing!" Josh squeaked.

"Following the ghost," she said.

"Are you crazy?" Josh said. "What if ghosts don't

like kids?"

"Gee, Josh," Dink said. "I thought you didn't believe in ghosts."

"Unless I see one with my own eyes," Josh said, "and I just did! Let's get out of here!" The elevator door opened.

"Too late, Josh," Dink said. He and Ruth Rose pulled Josh into the elevator with them.

Dink pushed the button marked 2. "We'll check each floor," he said.

When the door opened on the second floor, the hallway was empty.

"Two more floors," Ruth Rose said, pushing the number 3 button.

But they didn't see the ghost on the third or fourth floor, either.

"There are no more floors," Dink said, looking at the panel of buttons.

"Good, let's go home!" Josh said.

"What's this one for?" Ruth Rose asked, pointing to a black button without a number.

"Maybe you push it for emergencies," Dink said.

She shook her head. "Nope. This red one says EMERGENCY."

Dink shrugged. "There's only one way to find out," he said. He pushed the black button. The elevator creaked, then slowly started moving up.

"I'm having a nightmare," Josh mumbled. "I'm not really chasing a ghost around a hotel. Any minute, I'm gonna wake up in bed!"

"Don't worry, Josh," Ruth Rose said with a grin. "I'll protect you."

The elevator stopped with a gentle thud.

When the doors opened, the ghost was waiting for them.

"It followed us!" Josh screamed, jumping behind Ruth Rose.

"No, you followed me!" the ghost said. "What do you want?"

Behind the white figure, a door opened. A stooped, gray-haired man stepped into the hall.

The ghost pointed a thin finger at the kids. "They followed me up here, Ebenezer."

The man chuckled and shuffled toward the open

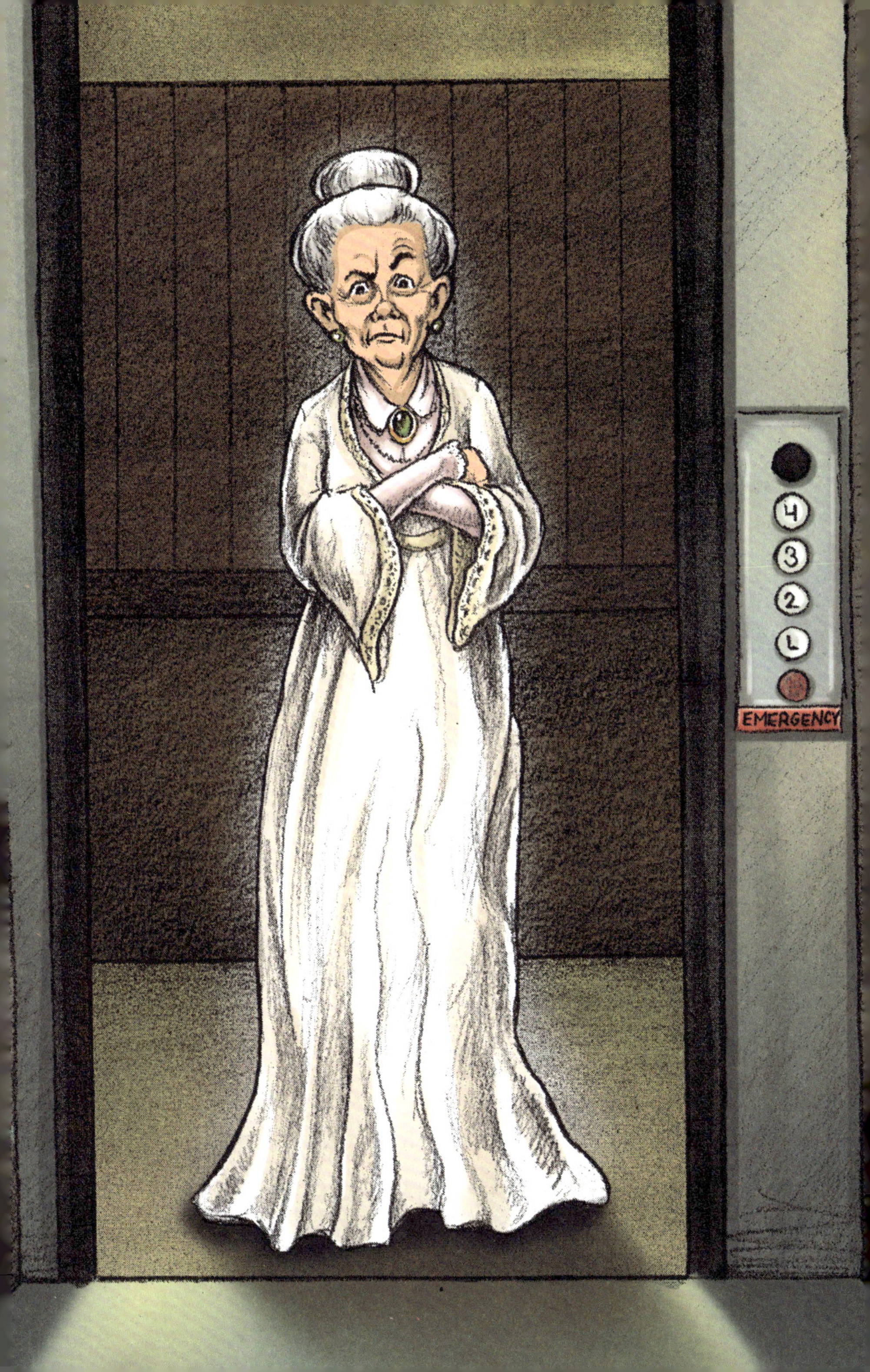
4
3
2
L
EMERGENCY

elevator. "Well, perhaps we should keep them!"

"NO!" Josh yelled from behind Ruth Rose. "Please let us go!"

Dink stared at the figure in white. Where had he seen that face before? Suddenly he remembered. She was the woman in the picture on Mr. Linkletter's desk!

Dink stepped out of the elevator. "Hello, Mr. and Mrs. Spivets," he said. "I'm Dink Duncan and these are my friends Josh and Ruth Rose."

"How d'you do," the man said, peering at Dink. His eyes were the color of blueberries. "You must be the three children our nephew told us about."

Josh peeked at Mrs. Spivets from behind Ruth Rose. "You mean she's not the ghost?" he asked.

"Of course I'm not the ghost!" Mrs. Spivets said. "Ebenezer, shall we invite these three in for cookies?"

"Of course, my love." The old man smiled at the kids. "Come along, kiddos!"

The kids followed Mr. and Mrs. Spivets through a small hallway and into an old-fashioned parlor.

Sunlight poured into the room. Through tall

windows, the kids could see treetops across Main Street.

Dink looked around the room. The walls were covered with paintings, and he'd never seen so many books!

Mrs. Spivets came in carrying a tray. "Please sit," she told the kids. She handed each of them a glass of milk. Her husband bustled in with a cookie jar shaped like a rooster. He pulled off the rooster's head.

"Cookie?" he said.

Each of the kids took one cookie.

"Now then," Mr. Spivets said as he sat next to his wife, "what are you kids up to?"

"We read about the ghost in the newspaper," Ruth Rose said.

"And we came to see it," Dink said.

"But we didn't!" Josh added.

"Then Mr. Linkletter told us how the ghost is ruining the hotel's business," Ruth Rose continued. "So we've decided to investigate!"

Mrs. Spivets stared at the kids. "Investigate?" she said. "Like detectives?"

"Right," Dink said. "Did you see the ghost?" he asked Mrs. Spivets.

She looked at her husband. "No, but we've heard it, haven't we, dear?"

He nodded. "Two nights in a row! Dreadful noises coming from the walls. And a voice calling out my name! 'Ebenezer,' it said, 'go away, go away!'"

Josh gulped. "It knew your name?"

"The voice spoke to me, too," Mrs. Spivets said. "It said, 'Flo, leave this place!'"

She began to cry into a lace hanky.

Mr. Spivets patted his wife's hand. "We've just made a difficult decision," he told the kids. "We're going to sell the hotel. Some real estate company in New York wants to buy it."

"Sell the Shangri-la!" Dink blurted.

"But you can't!" Ruth Rose said.

"We were going to leave the Shangri-la to our nephew," Mrs. Spivets said. "But now…"

"Now it looks as if the hotel will go to Eatch, Rail, and Roock," Mr. Spivets said.

"Who are they?" Ruth Rose asked.

"They're the three partners in the real estate company," Mr. Spivets said. "They've been after us to sell for months."

He crossed to a small desk and pulled out a letter. "They want to tear down the Shangri-la and build a highrise in its place!" he said.

Mr. Spivets placed the letter on the tea tray. "Mrs. Spivets and I don't want to sell, but we don't know what else to do. Somehow we feel as if we've failed our guests."

He looked down at his wife. "I telephoned the real estate people this morning. They will be here tomorrow with papers for us to sign."

Mrs. Spivets looked up. Her eyes were red. "Isn't there anything else we can do?" she asked.

Ebenezer Spivets took his wife's hand in his. "I would do anything for you, dear, but I'm too old to fight ghosts."

"Well, we're not!" Dink said, springing to his feet. "We'll find the ghost and get rid of it, too!" He looked at Josh and Ruth Rose. "Right, guys?"

"Right!" Ruth Rose said.

Mr. Spivets beamed. "You're hired!" he said.

Josh groaned. "Can I have another cookie?" he asked.

Chapter 4

"How are we gonna get rid of a ghost?" Josh asked in the elevator. "Even if I did believe in it."

"I don't know yet," Dink answered. "But we can't let those real estate guys tear down the Shangri-la!"

The elevator door slid open. Mr. Linkletter was standing behind his desk, just staring into space.

"Let's go to my house," Dink whispered. "We can make a plan while we eat."

"Yes!" Josh said. "Those cookies weren't big enough to fill up a flea!"

Dink laughed. "Not everyone has a stomach like the Grand Canyon, Josh!"

They headed up Main Street, then followed Silver Circle around the school to Dink's house.

Dink got out the peanut butter and bread. Josh found a bag of pretzels. Ruth Rose poured milk for everyone.

"Make my sandwich extra fat," Josh ordered. "I'm fainting from hunger!"

Dink pushed the peanut butter and bread toward Josh. "I'm not your servant, your royal highness!"

Josh grinned and began building his sandwich.

"Okay," Dink said, sitting at the table. "How do you get rid of a ghost?"

"First you have to prove that there is one," Josh said, taking a big bite of his sandwich.

"You still don't believe there's a ghost at the hotel?" Ruth Rose asked.

Josh swallowed and shook his head. "Nope."

He lined up four pretzels on the table. "We talked

酒店奇异事件

to Livvy, but she hadn't seen the ghost," Josh said. He picked up a pretzel and ate it.

"Then we asked Mr. Linkletter if he'd seen the ghost, but he said he hadn't." Josh ate another pretzel.

He picked up the last two pretzels. "Mr. and Mrs. Spivets didn't see the ghost either, they just heard noises!"

Josh popped the pretzels into his mouth. "Guys," he said as he chewed, "nobody we talked to saw the ghost. So maybe there is no ghost!"

Dink and Ruth Rose stared at Josh.

"He's right," Ruth Rose said after a minute. "Everyone we talked to said someone else had seen the ghost."

"So what should we do?" Dink asked.

"We have to see the ghost for ourselves," Ruth Rose said.

Dink blinked. "But how do we do that?" he asked.

Josh licked peanut butter from his fingers. "Well, we could start by finding someone who really did see

117

the ghost."

"But everyone who saw it checked out of the hotel," Ruth Rose said.

Dink swallowed the last of his sandwich. "We have to talk to those people," he said. "Maybe Mr. Linkletter will help us."

"Good idea," Ruth Rose said. "Let's go back to the hotel."

"No dessert?" Josh asked.

"Wipe off your milk mustache and come on!" Dink said.

The kids hurried back to the hotel. Mr. Linkletter looked up as the kids came in. "I hear you had a chat with my aunt and uncle," he said.

"They hired us to get rid of the ghost!" Dink informed him.

The corners of Mr. Linkletter's mouth wiggled. It was almost a smile. "And do you have a plan?"

"Sort of," Ruth Rose said. "But we need the names and phone numbers of the guests who saw the ghost."

Mr. Linkletter shook his head. "Sorry. Our guests, even the ones who leave, pay for privacy."

酒店奇异事件

"Well, are there any guests left at all?" she asked.

Mr. Linkletter pointed to a man and woman reading in a corner of the lobby. "Mr. and Mrs. Jeffers haven't checked out. But I don't know if they saw the ghost."

"Let's go ask them!" Dink said. He headed across the lobby.

The man was wearing jeans, hiking boots, and a white sweater.

The woman had black hair and wore a dark blue sweater and faded jeans.

"Hi, Mr. and Mrs. Jeffers," Dink said. "My name is

Dink. These are my friends Josh and Ruth Rose. We're investigating the ghost. Did you see it?"

"Why do you want to know?" the man asked.

"Because the hotel owners have hired us to get rid of it!" Ruth Rose said.

"If there really is a ghost," Josh muttered.

"There is!" Mrs. Jeffers said. "It scared me half to death!"

"So you saw it?" Dink asked.

"We both did," Mr. Jeffers said, setting down his book. "Last night we played cards down here until about midnight. When we went up to our room, this thing appeared out of nowhere!"

Mrs. Jeffers shuddered. "The hallway seemed to grow cold!" she said.

"What did it look like?" Ruth Rose asked.

Mr. Jeffers closed his eyes. "The ghost kind of shimmered as she walked. She had wild-looking white hair and a long glowing robe."

"And black holes instead of eyes!" Mrs. Jeffers added.

"You said 'she,'" Ruth Rose said. "Was it a girl

酒店奇异事件

ghost?"

Mr. Jeffers looked at Ruth Rose. "Um, well, I guess so. At least the robe looked like a woman's."

"And you said the ghost 'walked', " Dink said. "Did it have feet?"

"Feet?" Mr. Jeffers said. "I'm not sure. We hurried right into our room."

Just then Mr. Linkletter came over to the sofa. "Excuse me, Dink," he said. "My uncle is on the phone."

"Mr. Spivets wants to talk to me?" Dink said.

Mr. Linkletter nodded. Dink followed him to the phone.

"Hello?" Dink said. He listened for a few minutes, then hung up and walked back to Josh and Ruth Rose.

"You're not gonna believe this," he said.

"Don't tell me they saw the ghost!" Josh said.

"Nope, but now we might," Dink said. "Mr. Spivets wants us to sleep in the hotel tonight!"

Chapter 5

Josh and Ruth Rose stared at Dink.

"Honest," Dink said.

"But why?" Ruth Rose asked.

"Since the hotel is almost empty, he said we'd be doing him a favor," Dink said. "If people see us here, they might think the ghost was just a joke."

"Let's do it!" Josh said. "I need a night away from the twins!"

Dink grinned. "Mr. Spivets invited our families, too. And he wants us to investigate the ghost while we're here!"

Josh laughed. "When my little brothers get here, that ghost better watch out!"

By suppertime it was all arranged. The three families would spend the night at the Shangri-la.

Ruth Rose's little brother, Nate, wanted to meet the ghost.

"He'll be my friend!" Nate said. "We can play with my dinosaurs together!"

Dink's family and Ruth Rose's family rode together in one car.

The Pintos' car was already in the parking lot when they arrived. Josh was holding on to his twin brothers, Brian and Bradley. The boys hugged twin teddy bears.

After locking the cars, all twelve of them trooped into the Shangri-la. Mr. and Mrs. Spivets were waiting in the lobby. They were all dressed up, as if it was a special occasion.

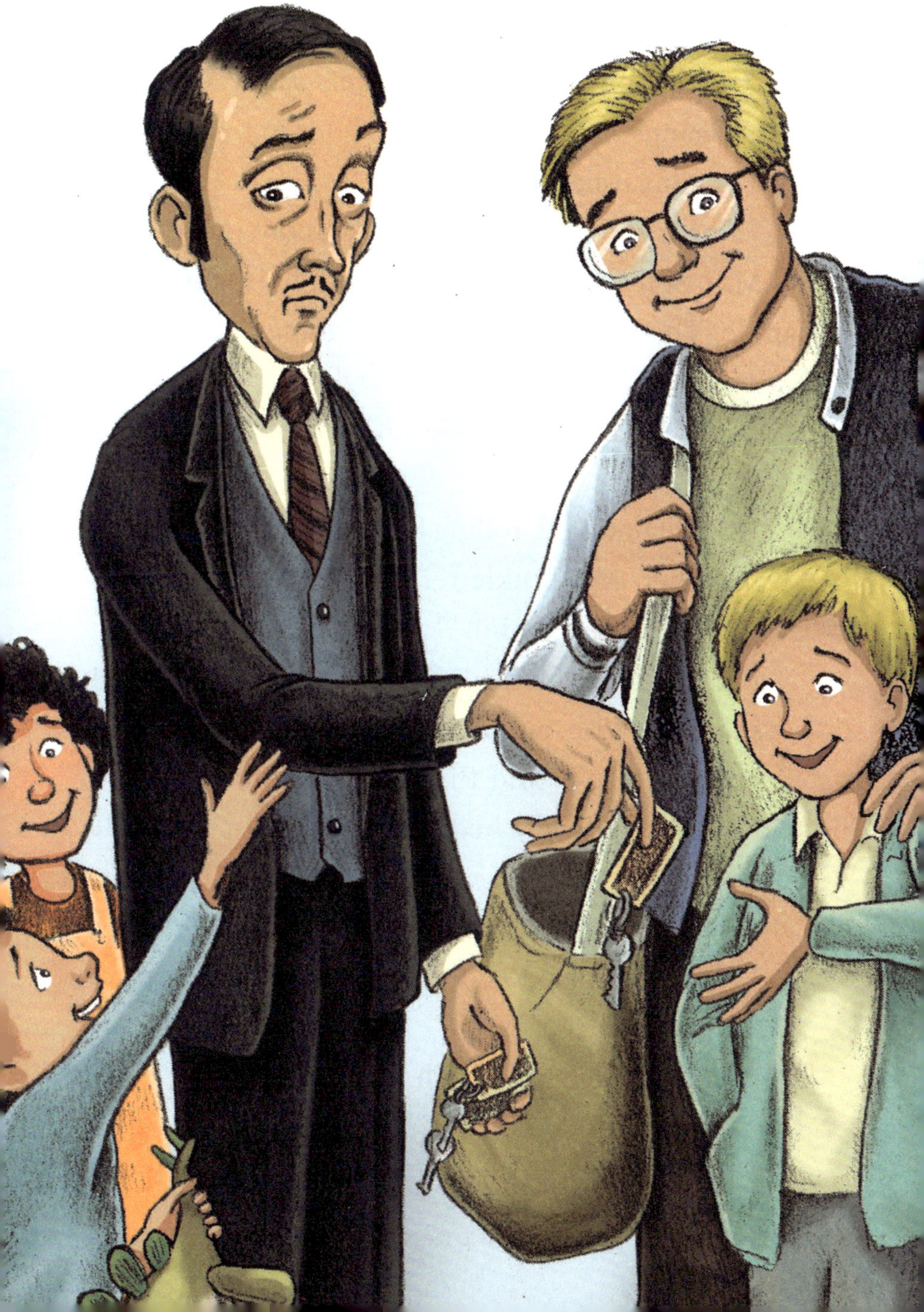

"Good evening, all!" Mr. Spivets said. "Welcome to the Shangri-la!"

The adults shook hands.

"This is very nice of you," Dink's mom told them.

Mrs. Spivets smiled at the kids. "It's the least we can do. These three detectives are going to get to the bottom of this ghost business tonight!"

Dink's father grinned. "As long as they do it before bedtime!"

"Dad," Dink said, rolling his eyes.

Just then Mr. Linkletter joined them. "Where's Casper?" Nate asked him. "I wanna see the ghost!"

Mr. Linkletter blinked at Nate, then handed room keys to Dink, Josh, and Ruth Rose.

"I think you'll find the rooms comfortable," he said. "I had rollaway beds brought in for the little ones."

Dink led them all to the elevator.

"What number do you guys have?" Josh asked. "We're in Room 203."

"I'm across the hall," Ruth Rose said, "in 204."

"Me too," Dink said. "202."

Five minutes later, all three families were in their rooms. Dink dumped his backpack on a narrow rollaway bed.

The room was pretty big, with a color TV and a miniature refrigerator. Dink opened the door and found a bunch of soft drinks and snacks.

"Can we eat this stuff?" Dink asked.

His father gave him a look. "You just finished supper, Dinko!"

Dink grinned. "Yeah, I know. How late can I stay up?"

"Nine o'clock," his mother said. "Remember, tomorrow is Monday."

"Mom, tomorrow's Columbus Day!" Dink said, grinning. "No school!"

"Okay, ten o'clock, but not a minute later!"

Dink left the room and knocked on Josh's door. "Come in!" one of the twins yelled.

Dink opened the door. The Pintos' room was even bigger than his. Three small beds were lined up opposite one big one.

Brian and Bradley wore matching Batman

jammies and were coloring in their coloring books.

Josh was standing in front of their little fridge, tossing down peanuts.

"Can Josh come out and play?" Dink said, grinning.

Josh's dad said, "Sure, just be back by breakfast time."

Josh laughed. "Let's get Ruth Rose," he said to Dink.

They walked to Room 204 and knocked. Ruth Rose opened the door and stepped out. "My folks are trying to get Nate to go to bed," she whispered.

"Let's go down to the lobby and think of a plan," Dink suggested.

"I already have one!" Ruth Rose announced.

"You do?" Dink said.

Ruth Rose nodded. "Mr. Linkletter told us the ghost showed up at midnight, right? Mr. and Mrs. Jeffers said the same thing."

Josh snorted. "So what's your plan, to hang out and say hi to the ghost when the clock strikes twelve?"

Ruth Rose grinned. "Exactly!"

Chapter 6

"It smells awful in here," Josh muttered.

"Josh, this closet is filled with cleaning stuff," Dink told him. "It's supposed to smell awful."

"Could you guys whisper?" Ruth Rose said. "You want our parents to wake up and find us gone?"

It was nearly midnight. Ten minutes before, the kids had snuck out of their rooms and hidden in the closet.

Josh yawned. "I should be asleep, having a great dream," he said. "Instead, I'm squashed in here like a sardine, waiting for a dumb ghost who isn't even real!"

Dink grinned in the dark. "I heard that ghosts hate kids with red hair," he whispered.

"Yeah? Well, I heard that ghosts eat blond-haired kids for breakfast!"

Suddenly Ruth Rose put out both hands. "Shh, I think I heard something," she said.

Josh snorted. "Nice try, Ruth Rose, but…"

"Shh!" whispered Dink. "I heard something, too!"

He pushed the closet door open a crack. All three kids peered out into the hallway.

Dink heard a groan, like the wind howling through a cave.

Suddenly a tall white figure appeared at the end of the hall. It gave off a shimmery white light and seemed to float above the floor.

"Oh my gosh!" Josh croaked. "I wanna go back to bed!"

The ghost wore a long white gown. Its hair was

white and stuck up in spikes. And there were just black, empty holes where the eyes should have been!

Josh grabbed Dink's arm. It hurt, but Dink was too scared to say anything.

The figure drifted slowly toward the kids' hiding place. It was carrying a long silver sword.

"It knows we're in here!" Josh squeaked.

The ghost paused at each door, then stopped in front of Room 202.

That's our room! Dink thought.

"Diiiiinnnnk," the ghost moaned. "Goooo hooooome! Thiiiis plaaace is daaaangerous!"

Every hair on Dink's head stood up. He felt cold, as if someone had opened a window.

The ghost floated to the next room.

This time it moaned, "Josssh, go hooome. Leave before it's toooo laaate!"

Outside Room 204, the ghost moaned its final message: "Ruth Rose, take your faaamily and leave nooow!"

Then the ghost drifted back the way it had come. Seconds later, the hallway was empty.

A to Z 神秘案件

Ruth Rose jumped up and shoved the door open. "Come on, let's see where it went!" she said.

"Who cares where it went!" Josh said. "I'm outta here!"

"Come on, Josh," Dink said. "I promised Mr. and Mrs. Spivets we'd get rid of the ghost. And we only have till morning!"

酒店奇异事件

"But what if it gets rid of us instead!"

Dink grabbed Josh's arm and started down the hall. He stopped and listened at Room 202. He heard his father snoring, and grinned.

Suddenly Josh stuck his nose in the air. "What's that smell?" he said.

Dink shrugged and kept walking.

Ruth Rose had reached the end of the hall. "It disappeared," she said when they were standing together.

"I smell it here, too," Josh said.

"Smell what?" Ruth Rose asked.

"I don't know," Josh said. "But it reminds me of something."

Around the corner, the kids found a gray metal door. A red sign on the door read FIRE EXIT.

"Maybe it went through there!" Ruth Rose whispered, pointing at the door.

Dink held his breath, then slowly pushed the door open. The kids peered into the stairwell. They saw dark steps going up and down.

"Should we split up and check it out?" Dink asked.

"No way!" Josh said. "We stick together!"

Dink grinned at his friend. "Still think the ghost is a joke?"

Josh made a face at Dink.

"Guys," Ruth Rose said. "How did the ghost know our names and which rooms we were in?"

"Maybe it has supernatural powers!" Josh said.

"Or maybe the ghost is really someone in the hotel," Dink added. "Someone who knows us!"

Ruth Rose nodded. "I think the ghost came out tonight looking just for us."

"You mean to scare us away, like it did the other

people?" Dink asked.

Ruth Rose nodded again.

"Well, it worked!" Josh said. "Let's hit the trail!"

"Hey, what's this?" Ruth Rose asked. She plucked a white hair off the doorframe.

Dink examined the hair. "The ghost had white hair like this," he said.

"Yeah," Ruth Rose said, "but ghosts don't lose hair, people do!"

Suddenly the door to Room 204 opened. Ruth Rose's father popped his head out. "Okay, you guys, time to hit the sack."

"But, Dad, we just…" Ruth Rose said.

Her father shook his head. "Say good night to the boys, Ruth Rose. Now."

Chapter 7

By nine the next morning, the three families were down in the lobby. Ruth Rose's parents had treated them all to breakfast at Ellie's Diner, then they'd walked back to the hotel for their luggage.

While the adults thanked Mr. Linkletter and the Spivetses, the kids huddled on the sofa.

"What're we gonna do?" Dink asked. "Mr. and Mrs. Spivets are selling the hotel today!"

Ruth Rose pulled the white hair from her pocket. "This proves that someone is just pretending to be the ghost," she said. "But we don't know who or why!"

"Maybe one of the guests has white hair," Josh said.

"Josh, all the guests are gone except Mr. and Mrs. Jeffers, and they both have dark hair," Ruth Rose reminded him.

"Could the hair be from a wig?" Dink asked. "The ghost could have been wearing a costume and makeup."

"That's it!" Josh cried. "Last night I smelled makeup in the hall. I remember the yucky smell from last Halloween!"

Just then Mr. Linkletter walked over to the kids. He looked even more unhappy than he had the day before.

"This is a sad day," Mr. Linkletter said. "Eatch, Rail, and Roock will be here at noon with the papers."

"NOON!" Ruth Rose jumped up. "Then we still have three hours!"

Mr. Linkletter gazed down at her. "I'm afraid it's

too late." He shook his head and walked away.

"We have to find out who's pretending to be the ghost," Ruth Rose said. "If we don't, Livvy and Mr. Linkletter will lose their jobs!"

"And Mr. and Mrs. Spivets will lose their home!" Dink added.

"Guys, I think I know who the ghost is," Josh said.

Dink and Ruth Rose stared at him.

"Well," Dink said. "Who?"

"The only people left in the hotel are Livvy, Mr. Linkletter, and his aunt and uncle, right?"

"Right," Ruth Rose said.

"And we know that none of them want the hotel to be torn down," Josh continued.

"You forgot about Mr. and Mrs. Jeffers," Dink said. "They're still here."

Josh grinned. "Bingo!"

"The Jefferses?" Ruth Rose said. "But they said they saw the ghost outside their room."

"Sure they saw the ghost," Josh said. "One of them is the ghost!"

"I know how we can find out," Dink said. "We

have to search their room."

"Mr. Linkletter will never let us do that," Josh said.

"Well, maybe he won't let us, but I know someone who might," Ruth Rose said.

"Who?" asked Dink.

"Livvy!"

The kids said good-bye to their families, then hurried to the door that led to the basement.

They found Livvy in a cozy room, drinking a cup of tea. She was wearing her maid's uniform. "'Morning, kids," she said. "What brings you down here?"

"We saw the ghost last night!" Ruth Rose said.

Livvy's eyes widened. "Really? Where? Tell me!"

The kids explained about spending the night in the hotel and hiding in the cleaning closet.

"It was so creepy!" Josh said. "First we heard all these weird noises, then this thing came out of nowhere!"

"It glowed!" Ruth Rose said. She showed Livvy the white hair. "And we found this!"

"We think the ghost is one of the guests wearing a

costume and wig," Dink explained.

Suddenly Livvy let out a gasp. "It was a wig!" she cried.

"What was?" Ruth Rose asked.

"I just remembered," Livvy said. "Yesterday I was in 301 getting ready to vacuum. When I looked under the bed for shoes and stuff, I saw this hairy white thing. I thought it was a rat. But it could have been a white wig!"

"Who's in Room 301?" Dink asked.

Livvy shrugged. "I don't know their name, but they're a nice couple from New York."

"Could you let us in so we could check the room for clues?" Ruth Rose asked.

Livvy shook her head. "Sorry, but you know how Mr. Linkletter is about the guests' privacy."

"But Mr. and Mrs. Spivets hired us to get rid of the ghost!" Dink said. "Besides, if they have to sell the hotel, you and Mr. Linkletter will lose your jobs!"

"And Mr. and Mrs. Spivets will have to move," Ruth Rose added. "Please, Livvy? It won't take us long."

Livvy took a moment to think. "Okay," she finally said. "But just for two minutes!"

"Hey, what's this?" Josh had stuck his head into a small opening in one wall.

"That's an old dumbwaiter," Livvy explained. "In the old days, the hotel sent food up to the guests. Each room had one of these little elevator things. When the food got up there, the guests just opened a door and pulled out their food tray."

"Our room didn't have one," Dink said.

"None of them do anymore," Livvy said. "When the hotel closed its kitchen, the dumbwaiters were all sealed up."

She pointed to the one in her wall. "That's the only hole left."

Josh stuck his head back into the opening. "Cool! This thing goes way up!"

"Right," Livvy explained. "The shaft is still there, but the openings into the rooms were covered over."

Josh yelled "Hello!" into the empty shaft. His voice came echoing back.

Livvy finished her tea. "Okay, let's go," she said. "I'll be glad when Mr. Linkletter is back to normal again. He's even grouchier than usual!"

Livvy took the kids up to the third floor, then knocked at Room 301. When no one answered, she unlocked the door and pushed it open.

"Please don't touch anything," she said. She knelt down and peeked under both beds. "The wig's gone!"

The kids looked around the room. "Maybe it's in the closet!" Ruth Rose whispered.

Livvy pulled open the closet door. On the top shelf sat a plastic head wearing a spiky white wig.

"That's it!" Josh said.

"Can you take it down?" Dink asked.

A to Z 神秘案件

Livvy carefully took the head down and set it on a table.

Ruth Rose removed the white hair from her pocket and held it next to the wig. "The hairs are the same!" she said.

Chapter 8

"Look." Dink pointed to a small framed picture on the bedside table. "Mr. and Mrs. Jeffers!"

"You know these people?" Livvy asked.

"We met them yesterday," Ruth Rose said. "We think one of them might be the ghost."

Livvy's eyes grew wide. "Why would they want to scare the guests away? They seem so nice!"

"That's what we plan to find out," Dink said.

Livvy carefully placed the wig back on the closet shelf.

As she stepped back, her arm caught on something. A long silver object clunked to the floor.

"It's the ghost's sword!" Ruth Rose said. She picked it up and laughed. "It's just painted wood!"

"Guys, look at this stuff!" Josh had been examining some tubes and bottles on a vanity table. "Look, white clown makeup. And black! This is what I smelled in the hallway last night!"

"Hey, guys, a tape recorder," Ruth Rose said.

"Kids, please don't touch…"

Before Livvy could finish, Ruth Rose had pushed the PLAY button. Suddenly the room was filled with spooky noises. Livvy and the kids listened as a voice moaned and groaned.

"Those are the same noises we heard last night!" Dink said.

"Have you seen Mr. and Mrs. Jeffers this morning?" Ruth Rose asked Livvy.

147

Livvy shook her head. "Maybe they went out for breakfast." She looked at her watch. "And I have to get busy."

Livvy locked the door behind them, and they all got in the elevator.

"Thanks for letting us in," Ruth Rose said to Livvy.

Livvy put one finger to her lips. "Let's keep this a secret, okay?" she whispered. "From you-know-who!"

"It's a deal," Ruth Rose whispered back.

The elevator door opened and Livvy left the kids in the lobby.

"There's Mr. Linkletter," Josh said. "Maybe he knows where Mr. and Mrs. Jeffers went."

The kids walked over to the front desk.

Mr. Linkletter looked as if he hadn't been to bed. His suit was rumpled, and his hair stuck up in the back.

"Maybe we shouldn't disturb him," Ruth Rose whispered.

"But we have to find Mr. and Mrs. Jeffers," Dink said. "We don't have much more time!"

Dink walked up to the desk and put on his best

smile. "Hi, Mr. Linkletter!"

Mr. Linkletter gazed down at Dink. "Oh, hello," he said.

"Do you happen to know where Mr. and Mrs. Jeffers are this morning?" he asked.

Mr. Linkletter waved his hand toward the door. "They told me they were going to Ellie's for breakfast."

"Thanks, Mr. Linkletter!" Dink said.

The kids left the hotel and hurried up Main Street toward Ellie's Diner.

"What're we gonna say to them?" Josh asked. "We can't just walk up and accuse them of being the ghost, can we?"

Ruth Rose pushed open the door to the diner. "Don't worry," she said. "I have a plan."

Ellie was behind the counter, mixing tuna salad in a big bowl. She waved as the kids sat in one of the booths.

"There they are," Josh whispered. He nodded his head toward another booth, where Mr. and Mrs. Jeffers were eating breakfast.

"They look so nice," Dink said. "Not like people

who would try to ruin a hotel."

Ellie came to their booth. "Back so soon?" she asked, opening her pad. "Don't tell me you're having another breakfast!"

"Can I borrow your pad and pencil?" Ruth Rose asked.

Ellie gave Ruth Rose a sly smile and handed them over. "What are you kids up to?" she asked.

"I'll give them back in a minute," Ruth Rose said.

"Okey-dokey, I'll see you in a minute then," Ellie said, heading back to her tuna salad.

Ruth Rose began writing.

"What're you doing?" Josh asked.

"Wait a sec!" Ruth Rose said. She finished and pushed the pad in front of Dink and Josh. "What do you think?"

DEAR MR. AND MRS. JEFFERS,
   WE KNOW ALL ABOUT THE WHITE WIG AND THE TAPE RECORDER.
                    GUESS WHO!

"Ruth Rose! What if we're wrong about the Jefferses?" Dink asked.

"We're not wrong," Ruth Rose said, getting up.

She walked over to Ellie, said something to her, and handed her the pad. Ellie smiled at Ruth Rose, then headed for the Jefferses' booth.

Ruth Rose hurried back and sat down. "Now watch," she told Dink and Josh.

They watched as Ellie handed the note to Mrs. Jeffers.

Mrs. Jeffers read the note, then said something to Ellie. Ellie pointed toward the kids.

Mrs. Jeffers waved, and Ruth Rose waved back.

"Come on," Ruth Rose said. She walked over to the Jefferses' booth. Dink and Josh were right behind her.

"Hi!" Ruth Rose said, pulling the white hair from her pocket. "I think your wig got caught on the fire door last night. You left this."

She placed the white hair on the green place mat.

Mrs. Jeffers stared at the hair, then at the kids.

Finally she looked at her husband.

Mr. Jeffers sighed, then grinned at the kids. "Looks like you got us!" he said.

Chapter 9

"So you really are the ghost?" Ruth Rose asked.

Mr. Jeffers nodded. "That was me last night," he said. "Cindy here was the ghost the first two nights."

He looked at the kids. "Weren't you asleep in your rooms when I came by?"

"We hid in a smelly closet and saw you!" Josh said.

Mr. Jeffers smiled. "Do I make a good ghost?"

"You sure scared me!" Josh said.

A to Z 神秘案件

"But why did you do it?" Ruth Rose asked.

"We're both actors, and we're broke," Mrs. Jeffers said. "A few weeks ago, three men came up to us after a rehearsal and asked if we wanted a job."

"So we told them sure!" her husband said. "The men told us to check into the Shangri-la and scare the guests away. We came up with the ghost costume ourselves."

"How do you make it glow?" Josh asked.

"I glued a string of tiny lights inside the gown," Mrs. Jeffers said. "The battery was under the wig."

Her husband smiled. "And I thought of hiding the tape recorder in the basement dumbwaiter. The noise went all through the hotel walls!"

"But that's so mean!" Ruth Rose said. "If the hotel closes, what will happen to Mr. Linkletter and Livvy and Mr. and Mrs. Spivets?"

Mr. Jeffers put up his hands. "Who said anything about the hotel closing?"

"Mr. and Mrs. Spivets did," Dink said. "They're selling the hotel because of you!"

"What?" Mrs. Jeffers said. "But Mr. and Mrs.

酒店奇异事件

Spivets are supposed to know all about the ghost act. So is Mr. Linkletter."

"Look," said Mr. Jeffers. "The three guys who hired us told us that the hotel is going to be used in a horror movie. Scaring guests away is supposed to be great publicity. All the guests are going to get their money back, plus free passes to the movie."

"And we're supposed to get starring parts in the movie!" his wife said. "It's a big break for us!"

The kids looked at each other.

"But Mr. and Mrs. Spivets don't know anything about any movie," Ruth Rose said. "Neither does Mr. Linkletter. They're really upset because they're going to have to sell the hotel. Today!"

"Yeah," Josh said. "Mrs. Spivets was crying and everything!"

"We even saw the letter from the real estate company," Dink said. "Their names were something like Peach or Roach."

"Eatch, Rail, and Roock?" Mr. Jeffers suddenly asked.

"That's them!" Dink said. "They've been trying to buy the hotel for a long time, but Mr. Spivets refused to sell. Until now."

Mr. Jeffers looked at his wife. "Oh, no," he said. "Eatch, Rail, and Roock are the men who hired us!"

His wife had gone from happy to sad. "No wonder they told us not to talk to Mr. Linkletter about the movie. There never was one!"

Her husband shook his head. "All they wanted was the hotel—and we helped them get it!"

"I feel terrible," Mrs. Jeffers said. She turned to her husband. "Todd, isn't there anything we can do?"

Mr. Jeffers looked at the kids. "Do you think it's too late?" he asked. "Have they actually sold the hotel yet?"

Dink glanced at the clock over the counter. "They're signing the papers at noon," he said. "But I think I know how you can get rid of Eatch, Rail, and Roock and save the hotel at the same time!"

Chapter 10

"This wig itches!" Josh complained. He, Dink, and Ruth Rose were hiding behind the desk in the hotel lobby.

Josh was dressed as the ghost, complete with wig, robe, and makeup.

"It won't be long now," Dink said, glancing at the clock. It was almost noon!

"Eatch, Rail, and Roock had better hurry up," Josh

said. "I'm gonna suffocate in this dumb dress!"

From where he was hiding, Dink could see the rest of the lobby. Mr. Linkletter was sitting on the sofa with his aunt and uncle.

On the other side of the lobby, Mr. and Mrs. Jeffers were playing cards with Linda Gomez, the reporter from the *Green Lawn Gazette*. Next to her sat a man with a camera.

"What if they don't come?" Ruth Rose whispered.

Dink smiled and pointed at the front door. "I think they just did!"

Three men walked into the lobby. One was tall, one was medium, and one was short and round. Each was dressed in a dark suit, white shirt, and blue tie.

"They look like three penguins!" Josh said.

Mr. Linkletter hurried over to the men, then led them back to his aunt and uncle.

The tall man shook hands with Mr. Spivets. "I am Fletcher Eatch," he said.

"I am Randolph Rail," the medium-sized man said, sticking out his hand.

"And I am Miles Roock," the short man said,

shaking hands in turn.

Mr. Spivets nodded at the men. "Have you brought the papers?" he asked.

Fletcher Eatch beamed. "We certainly have!" he said. He handed Mr. Spivets an important-looking document.

Randolph Rail removed an envelope from his briefcase. "And here's the check."

Miles Roock whipped a gold pen out of his pocket. "All we need is your signature, Mr. Spivets," he said.

Mr. Spivets looked sadly at his wife. Then he took the pen and started to sign the document.

Just then Mr. and Mrs. Jeffers walked up.

"Look, Todd!" Mrs. Jeffers said. "It's the movie

producers!"

"What a surprise," her husband said. "We were just talking about the movie you're going to film here in the hotel!"

Mr. Spivets paused. "What's this about a movie?" he asked suspiciously.

"Um…" began Fletcher Eatch.

"Well…" started Randolph Rail.

"W-we can explain!" said Miles Roock.

"There's no need to explain," said Linda Gomez. She stood up and walked toward the men. "I'm a reporter from the *Green Lawn Gazette*. Tomorrow my column will tell the whole town how you tried to trick these people into selling their hotel!"

The three men stared at Linda, then at the Jefferses. Finally their eyes landed on Mr. and Mrs. Spivets.

Fletcher Eatch turned pink.

Randolph Rail went white.

Miles Roock turned purple. There was dead silence in the Shangri-la lobby.

And then a ghost in a spiky white wig floated up

from behind the desk. "Go hooome," it moaned in a creepy voice. "Go home before it's toooo laaate!"

Everyone in the lobby—except Eatch, Rail, and Roock—started to laugh.

"I guess I won't be needing this," Mr. Spivets said. He ripped the document he was holding into pieces.

"W-what are you doing!" Fletcher Eatch spluttered.

"You agreed to sell this hotel!" Randolph Rail said.

"You can't back out of a deal with Eatch, Rail, and Roock!" said Miles Roock.

Mrs. Spivets stood up next to her husband.

"Eatch, Rail, and Roock?" she said. "You should rearrange the letters in your names to Cheat, Liar, and

Crook!"

"And now," Mr. Spivets said, "I think it's time for you gentlemen to leave."

Without another word, Mr. Linkletter escorted the three men to the front door.

The man with the camera followed, snapping one picture after another.

Everyone cheered. Flo Spivets cheered the loudest.

Mrs. Jeffers turned back to Mr. and Mrs. Spivets. "My husband and I are so sorry for what we did," she said. "Can you ever forgive us?"

"Of course we can, dear," Mrs. Spivets said.

"In fact," said Mr. Spivets, "you were such good ghosts, we'd like to invite you to do it again! One weekend a month, we'd like you to put on a 'Shangri-la Mystery' for our guests. What do you think?"

"That's a great idea," Mr. Jeffers said. "We can get some of our actor friends to help!"

The photographer snapped pictures of the Jefferses and the Spivetses.

"Wait till my readers hear about this!" Linda Gomez said, writing it all down on her pad.

Then Mr. Spivets turned to Dink, Josh, and Ruth Rose. "And speaking of mysteries, I want to thank our three super sleuths!"

He pulled three envelopes out of his pocket. "From the bottom of our hearts, Mrs. Spivets and I thank you," he said. He handed the envelopes to the kids. "Please open these before you go to bed."

The photographer snapped a picture as the kids blushed.

"Be sure to mention their names in the column," Mrs. Spivets said to Linda Gomez.

"My pleasure," Linda said. "Now, how about a few more pictures of the three kids?"

Dink and Ruth Rose looked into the camera and smiled.

"Wait!" Josh said, struggling out of the ghost costume. "I don't want my picture in the paper with this wig and dress on!"

Later that night, the kids met in Dink's living room.

Dink was holding Loretta in his lap. She was

nibbling on one of his shirt buttons.

Josh pulled out the envelope Mr. Spivets had given him. "Can we open these now?" he asked.

"He said before we go to bed, Josh," Dink said.

"This is before we go to bed!"

"Josh is right!" Ruth Rose said. "I'm dying to know what's in mine. Let's open them on the count of three, okay? One, two, three!"

"Oh golly, my great-aunt Molly!" Josh said. "Three plane tickets to Florida!"

Ruth Rose held up the contents of her envelope. "And three passes to Disney World!"

Dink gulped when he saw what was in his envelope. He pulled out three fifty-dollar bills and a note:

> Thank you for saving our hotel and solving another Shangri-la mystery! Say hi to Mickey and Goofy for us!
>
> Much gratitude,
> Eb and Flo Spirets

酒店奇异事件

Dink, Josh, and Ruth Rose jumped up and did a triple high-five.

Loretta crawled off the sofa. No one was looking, so she started chewing one of the fifty-dollar bills.

Text copyright © 1999 by Ron Roy
Illustrations copyright © 1999 by John Steven Gurney
All rights reserved under International and Pan-American Copyright Conventions.
Published in the United States by Random House, Inc., New York, and simultaneously
in Canada by Random House of Canada Limited, Toronto.

本书中英双语版由中南博集天卷文化传媒有限公司与企鹅兰登（北京）文化发展有限公司合作出版。

"企鹅"及其相关标识是企鹅兰登已经注册或尚未注册的商标。
未经允许，不得擅用。
封底凡无企鹅防伪标识者均属未经授权之非法版本。

© 中南博集天卷文化传媒有限公司。本书版权受法律保护。未经权利人许可，任何人不得以
任何方式使用本书包括正文、插图、封面、版式等任何部分内容，违者将受到法律制裁。

著作权合同登记号：字18-2023-258

图书在版编目（CIP）数据

酒店奇异事件：汉英对照 /（美）罗恩·罗伊著；
（美）约翰·史蒂文·格尼绘；曹幼南译. -- 长沙：湖
南少年儿童出版社，2024.10. --（A to Z神秘案件）.
ISBN 978-7-5562-7817-6

Ⅰ. H319.4
中国国家版本馆CIP数据核字第2024H1W905号

A TO Z SHENMI ANJIAN JIUDIAN QIYI SHIJIAN

A to Z神秘案件 酒店奇异事件

[美] 罗恩·罗伊 著　　[美] 约翰·史蒂文·格尼 绘　　曹幼南 译

责任编辑：唐 凌　李 炜	策划出品：李 炜　张苗苗　文赛峰
策划编辑：文赛峰	特约编辑：杜天梦
营销编辑：付 佳　杨 朔　周晓茜	封面设计：霍雨佳
版权支持：王媛媛	版式设计：马睿君
插图上色：河北传图文化	内文排版：马睿君

出 版 人：刘星保
出　　版：湖南少年儿童出版社
地　　址：湖南省长沙市晚报大道89号
邮　　编：410016
电　　话：0731-82196320
常年法律顾问：湖南崇民律师事务所　柳成柱律师
经　　销：新华书店
开　　本：875 mm × 1230 mm　1/32　　印　刷：三河市中晟雅豪印务有限公司
字　　数：91千字　　　　　　　　　　　　印　张：5.25
版　　次：2024年10月第1版　　　　　　　印　次：2024年10月第1次印刷
书　　号：ISBN 978-7-5562-7817-6　　　　定　价：280.00元（全10册）

若有质量问题，请致电质量监督电话：010-59096394　团购电话：010-59320018